STRONG M

Brain Science, Mind Hacks, Mindfulness and More:

People with **Strong Minds** inspire themselves and influence others to take daily action and overcome any difficulty to achieve success, happiness, personal growth & life-long fulfillment.

"You don't have to dream big or try to change the world, just decide to change 'your' world as it is right now".

Copyright © 2019 Reece Pye – All Rights Reserved
www.ReecePye.com

Changing Mindsets – Changing Results   www.ReecePye.com

WHAT OTHERS SAY ABOUT REECE

"Reece has the enviable ability to direct a positive, constructive path from any situation. We think of him as a mentor and often refer to some of the concepts he taught us as 'Reece-isms'. His professionalism is 'second-to-none". **Managing Director - National Marketing Agency**

"I've known Reece for over a decade... he has many outstanding attributes including highly attuned emotional intelligence, broad-spectrum business acumen, an insatiable appetite for helping others and is a powerhouse in strategic thinking". **Managing Director - Management Consulting Firm**

"I have seen firsthand how Reece inspires people to raise performance and recall one initiative he led that resulted in £1.7m incremental sales income and turned a good performance into a great one". **Head of Change Management - Global Telco**

"Reece is a unique diamond in the world... he listens, observes and then questions before offering advice and suggestions, clearly he is a master in coaching for performance and rest assured, always gets results". **Head of Special Accounts - Directory Publishers**

"Reece is absolutely the real deal and has an almost laser like focus when it comes to spotting, creating and then implementing a more strategic approach than many could hope to muster". **Managing Director - 3D Architectural Visualisation**

Changing Mindsets – Changing Results

PLAYBOOK TABLE OF CONTENTS

SUBJECT MATTER & SUB-SECTIONS

ABOUT YOUR AUTHOR 7

INTRODUCTION TO STRONG MINDS! 12
Self-Study Is A Powerful Tool For Developing A Strong Mind 13
What Is A Playbook? 17
What Will You Learn From This Playbook? 18
Mind Hack Example Number 1 - Thinking Inside The Box Might Surprise You! 19
Mind Hack Example Number 2 - There Are Three Sides To Every Story. .22

CHAPTER 1 - THE SECRET OF TRUE SUCCESS 27
The Gods In The Heavens Discuss Success 27
Success Is Not Where You Expect It To Be Found 29
Learn Easy – Learn Fast – Learn Well 30
How You can Go From Wannabe To Expert 33

CHAPTER 2 - PROGRAMMING OF THE HUMAN MIND 39
Understanding Why We Are, Who We Are & Where We Are Today! 39
We Are Conditioned People, Programmed Like Computers And Robots (Bots) 41
The Truth And Use It To Take Back Control Of Our Minds! 46

Changing Mindsets – Changing Results

CHAPTER 3 - THE POWER OF MIND HACKS 51

Benefits Of Mind Hacks 51

Why Are Mind Hacks Important For You? 52

Mind Hacks Help Make You Stronger And Smarter! 53

The Positive Impact Of Mind Hacks 54

Where Did Mind Hacks Originate? 55

CHAPTER 4 - KEY ELEMENTS OF BRAIN SCIENCE FOR MIND CONTROL 58

Understanding The Difference Between Our Brain And Our Mind. 58

The Brain And The Mind 58

What Neuroscience Is Telling Us About Our Brain Power 59

The Technological Backdrop – Mind Power In Perspective 60

In Two Minds 63

The Amygdala (And Emotional Hijacks) 68

Synapses (Neural Connections) – The Importance In Reprogramming. .. 71

Your Internal GPS, The Reticular Activating System (RAS) & WYFOYS. ..76

Your Collective Unconscious Storehouse 78

Key Take Aways: 80

CHAPTER 5 - WHO ARE YOU - WHERE ARE YOU? 83

Who You Are & Where You Are Right Now? 83

What Do You Stand For – Your Core Value System 86

Conflicting Values 87

Assessing Your Values 91

The Passion Paradox 96

Core Beliefs 98

Self-Motivation & How To Create It. 100

Who **A**re **Y**ou - **W**here **A**re **Y**ou (Way) Self-Assessments Templates ...105

CHAPTER 6 - REPROGRAMMING YOUR MIND, A NEW DIRECTION AND POSSIBLY, A NEW WAY OF LIFE 116

Where History Meets The Present And Future 116

The Four Core Methods For Re-Programming! 116

So Where Do We Begin With Re-Programming? 121

Near Death Experiences (NDE), - A Parallel Universe - The Truman Show 125

Mindfulness & Meditation 132

The Surprise Meditation From A Buddhist Session 133

The Truth About You 136

CHAPTER 7 - OVERCOMING OBSTACLES & BARRIERS TO SUCCESS 139

The Single Biggest Obstacle in your way 139

System Bugs & Debugging 141

Inner Peace Of Mind & Outer Success Is An Elimination Process 147

CHAPTER 8 - MOVING YOU 'FROM-TO' 149

Turn A Negative Frame Of Mind Into A Positive One, Instantly. 149

Your Emotions Needn't Stay Fixed And Here's Why. 151

This Is Where The 'From-To' Formula Can Work For Your Benefit. .. 154

'From-To' Templates 158

SO WHAT HAPPENS NOW? **161**

Summary & Success Essentials 161

The 'Six-Figure Success Essentials' Framework 163

Purpose For A Meaningful Life! 166

Heads Up: All website addresses were double checked at the time of publishing and they were all accurate and working. Should you find any that don't (they could have been changed by the source producers) please let me know at: reecepye@reecepye.com

ABOUT YOUR AUTHOR

REECE PYE – SUMMARY BACKGROUND

My earliest childhood memory is living in a near derelict house earmarked for demolition by the local government, with no bathroom and just an outside toilet. It wasn't the best start in life but my Mum took it because, the alternative was that my Sister, Brother and me would be put into separate children's homes.

I was raised in a small market town in North Hampshire in the South of England to a mother that was given up by her own mum, even though they lived in the same town. My mum was therefore raised by her grandmother, my great grandmother.

It was a small town and so my mum and her mum (my grandmother) used to see each other on occasion and say a brief 'hello' but there was no conversation as such between them.

As for my upbringing, whatever we missed out on in terms of money or luxuries, my mum made up for with love and support. We were raised on a strong foundation of morals, values and concern for others, traits passed down by her loving Grandmother. Importantly, they both instilled in us an attitude of not judging anyone by their background, race, creed, colour or any other differences from ourselves.

My Mum raised us on her own because my Father was an alcoholic and never lived with us for long periods due to frequent spells in prison. He was an intelligent man however but allowed his deep inner emotions, desires and demons to rule him so when he was home, emotional and physical abuse often came as part of the unwelcome package. A sad example of a father, he died in his early 40's from a drink and sleeping tablets overdose, although no one knows to this day if it was intentional.

I was a skinny, shy, insecure little kid with a bit of a temper but this was tamed thanks to the kindness and dedicated support of the coaches at my local boxing club, which I joined, aged 10. In 9 years there, I became county and regional champion year after year and also reached numerous national championship finals. I distinctly recall my physical education teacher asking me why I kept going because I'd never be a champion but luckily, I ignored him and became one anyway. I'd been taught the technical skills needed to reach the national finals but never the inner mind games or plays that are so vital to gaining the winners edge at the top level.

This was my first exposure to coaching and it's been a major part of my leadership style ever since. My boxing coaches taught me more about how to be a decent human being than anyone in business ever have. I will be forever grateful for their unconditional, dedicated support and kindness.

Changing Mindsets – Changing Results   *www.ReecePye.com*

This factor along with my ambition and deep desire to be a great father and husband first and successful in my career second, is where my journey to exploring, discovering and developing a **Strong Mind** began. From age 20, I started investing in myself, studying anything I could find on the 'inner psychology' of influence and leadership in business from the best in the world. I still study to this day and always will until the day I die, it interests me like no other subject.

Fast forward to today and I look back from being a kid brought up on the support of social services and a tough start in life to having enjoyed a career with many more ups than downs, although you need some of the downs to help you grow faster and stronger.

The career highlight for me was becoming a successful businessman and senior advertising executive within a FTSE 100, leading national sales teams to generate nearly £100m in revenues and being recognised with 'Outstanding Contribution & Achievement Awards' by bosses I respected as decent leaders themselves. This put me in the top 5% of earners in the UK and on occasions, close to or in the top 1%. Although money was never the real motivator for me, when you have it, it does make life easier for sure. But for me, it was always more about proving to myself that I was worth something. It was then and still is about personal satisfaction of being the best I could be, and throughout the process, continually looking to grow, to support my family well and contribute wherever I could to everyone I met.

I'm blessed to have a wonderful wife and 2 great children who are following their own paths in life and we live in a beautiful part of the world, a few minutes drive from the South Downs National Park to the north and beeches to the south.

I read many years ago that when you get to a certain level of success, it's not always about being better than others but being different, stand out for the right reasons. I've never really been comfortable following the crowd so this struck a chord with me. This has meant being strong enough in mind to be different from the masses of people stuck as middle of the road performers and earners in life, never high or low but playing it safe. I would never ever knock anyone in that group but it just didn't suit me.

Along the way, my wife and I have had our challenges and lost loved ones including our second child, which had a major impact on my thinking, where I've focused my attention and energies, and consequently, what's included within this interactive playbook. What you'll find here is the result of my extensive study of the brain and the mind, along with a combination of practical application, testing and refining of methods that have, if I may say, enabled me to stand out from the crowds as a decent, giving human being.

As an old saying goes *"The true measure of a man is not in what he gets in life but in what he gives"* and my hope for you is that I give you something valuable with which to take control of the full miracle powers of your mind and your life.

I can't say the ideas are all mine but you can be sure however, that I've taken what's been useful, discarded what I found to be ineffective and added what is uniquely ME so that you can do the same and apply in a way that is unique to YOU.

We're all just custodians of knowledge really and if we keep it ourselves, it's forever limited, i.e. it only becomes valuable when applied and shared so please pass it on to others

Yours Positively

Reece

INTRODUCTION TO STRONG MINDS!

THE COMPLETE GUIDE TO UNDERSTAND AND USE THE FULL MIRACLE POWER OF YOUR MIND, TO GET WHAT YOU WANT IN LIFE!

Traditionally, success has been defined by money, power and status but today, young people are defining it by new, more rounded standards built on achieving personal satisfaction, a deeper sense of inner fulfillment by making a difference not just to their own lives but society in general. This means that success can be determined by what YOU want it to be and can come in various forms. The old ways of moving up the corporate ladder to achieve leadership status is no longer as valid because anyone can be empowered to lead in what they choose to do. The world today requires that we adapt and utilise all of our potential talent in ways that suit our environments and us.

For example: Women entrepreneurs in particular are leading the way with smaller businesses that fit around their life and contribute to society, not the other way around. In the USA alone, women owned business are growing at 2.5 times the national average. Real power then, comes from being open minded, fluid, agile and making the right choices for yourself, being in control of your life and this lies in the self-assured ability to lead your life your way.

SELF-STUDY IS A POWERFUL TOOL FOR DEVELOPING A STRONG MIND

Studying Mind Training and Brain Science is a wise decision that will help you become even wiser, and the wiser your decisions, the better your outcomes. This means being willing to expose yourself to new truths, fresh ways of thinking and a different, stronger approach to managing your mind.

All truly successful people posses a strong element of open mindedness, which is not surprising because if they thought like everyone else, they'd only achieve what everyone else is achieving, which converts into average or nothing special.

A strong mind is **alert, calm** and **focused** so let's look at these three attributes in advance of delving deeper into specific methods for mind training and how it can help you build these or make them even stronger.

ALERT

Whether it be in commerce, industry, government of non-profit organisations today, they all seem to be looking for quick thinkers and fast actors but this can also be confused with haste at times. Alert means being fully awake and aware of your environment and situations so you really notice what's going on in and around you. Being alert enough to consider choices and decisions in rational ways and not be driven by reactive emotions. It means being wise in response to any difficult or potentially dangerous risks and importantly, capitalising on any unusual opportunities that present themselves.

CALM

Pressure is rife in work environments today and managing emotions in the face of adversity can be challenging. A calm mind is a controlled mind, it sees reality rather than perception or illusion and is characterised by an ability to think or respond accordingly. A calm mind is relaxed and takes the heat out of negative emotions before deciding on the right course of action. A calm mind is composed and able to switch off from the chaos that surrounds us at times, i.e. all the noise, information, interruptions and people that can put your nerves on edge.

FOCUSED

It's often the case that people who want to grow are creative individuals who will come up with lots of different ideas. However, chasing them all can distract attention away from the bigger, more rewarding plays. This risks a dilution of energy, resources and effectiveness, which can be crippling if your resources are limited and spread thin. Focus is therefore directing your attention, interest, or activity towards a particular aim and being able to stop, take a breath and say NO to ideas or opportunities that take you off track. Focus is about clarity when targeting your energy, mentally and physically. The words of the great and late world famous management consultant Peter Drucker will resonate with any and all adults today, whether they be mired inside a traditional corporate environment or living life inside lean start-ups. Paying attention to important things means not paying attention to all the rest of the noise that distracts you from the successes you seek.

"People are effective because they say 'no' this isn't for me. There is nothing so useless and doing efficiently that which should not be done at all"

Success in whatever this term means to you personally, begins in the 'mind' and all three inner elements on mind control are important but ultimately, any and all of these must lead to appropriate decisions and action, which are demonstrated through your 'behaviours' on the outside.

This interactive playbook is therefore designed as both education and guide on how to coach yourself with practical, workable solutions that you can put into action in the real world, today.

I learned many years ago that to be successful, you must understand not just what other successful people do but why and how they do it the way they do. I've therefore been interested in the inner-psychology of mankind for years and have seen all matter of material on each of the subjects covered within this playbook. Not anywhere however, have I come across all of these key elements of managing your mind

Changing Mindsets – Changing Results　　　　　　　*www.ReecePye.com*

in one single place and based on the practical experiences of using and passing them on to people who've worked for or alongside me in business during the last 20+ years.

I've had a good career and from tough beginnings, have led a privileged life. It's now time to pass on what works outstandingly well so that others can benefit from this knowledge too. My objective in writing this 'self-coaching' playbook is that it will act as the foundation for you to become the architect that designs and builds your life in the way you want it to look, mentally, emotionally, financially.

The reason why 'self-coaching' is so important is that it puts you in control and the reality is, you know yourself better than you may 'currently' think you do and certainly better than anyone else ever will.

The value I've gained from searching for nuggets that led me to the gold I wanted, not just gold as in income and wealth creation but gold as in the principles with which to live a gold star life far are now condensed into this one single interactive playbook for you to benefit from.

With this in mind, let me introduce you to the simple but effective concept of the playbook, a trusty companion that can make a measurable difference to how you live your life, who, how you develop yourself, how you can help others and what you could accomplish in life.

1. What is a playbook?

The phrase **Playbook** originally came about by way of a book containing a sports team's strategies and plays (especially in American football) with a document for everyone to refer to, pull from, and repeat in order to achieve their desired results, to win. I have included within this interactive playbook a number of video links that offer support to the knowledge I'm sharing so you can actually interact by 'playing the book' at certain points.

This playbook therefore reflects a plan and play to develop a **Strong Mind**; a set of tested and proven approaches to personal improvement that you can use to create your own unique version of you, regardless of whether you're starting out in adult life, at the mid-life stage and questioning 'what next' or older and looking for ways to attain greater peace of mind. Whilst success in life (which is whatever you decide it should be and not based on anyone else's terms) is of interest to every human being on this planet and can be a serious subject, It is also somewhat experimental in nature and should be fun so I want you to play around with the ideas and use what is specifically best for you. There will be some work involved but it's enjoyable work in self-study that sets you up to play your own game on the journey of self-understanding and development of a **Strong Mind**.

2. What will you learn from this playbook?

You will learn the 4 key aspects of how the brain works in very simple to understand ways and how you can use the real miracle power of your mind to manage the brain better, i.e. the brain and the mind are not the same and this playbook will explain why.

This may at first seem like a hard concept to grasp but that's because your old way of thinking still has a hold on you, whereas you will have new ways of thinking and looking at the world by the end, or even before the end of this playbook. I will introduce you to **'Six Simple Steps'** to help you challenge your thinking and if necessary, some of your values and beliefs, and change any that are not serving you well.

I will share my **'Six-Figure Success Essentials'** Framework, so called because it's the framework I used to earn six-figure incomes early in my business career, working almost part-time and enjoying time with my family and friends. And, you'll be exposed to many other simple methods and frameworks that you'll find easy to remember and implement. One of these key elements in re-training your mind is using the principles of Mind Hacks to convey an idea with quick, easy, digestible shortcuts (summary lessons or stories) that can easily be absorbed into the mind to create new connections in the brain in just a few minutes, and that will add knowledge to aid your success. Once received into your mind, they work effortlessly to interrupt the pattern of conventional (conditioned or pre-programmed) thinking to create more effective neural connections and thought patterns, more positive and productive emotions and ultimately, more successful outcomes.

A key point to make here is that any changes should be ones YOU want to make and not what you THINK others should ask of you. This program is about you! What follows in the next pages are two examples of how Mind Hacks (Brain Training) work and how you can begin to see things differently:

Mind Hack Example Number 1 - Thinking Inside The Box Might Surprise You!

In the 4 x 4 grid below, how many squares are there?

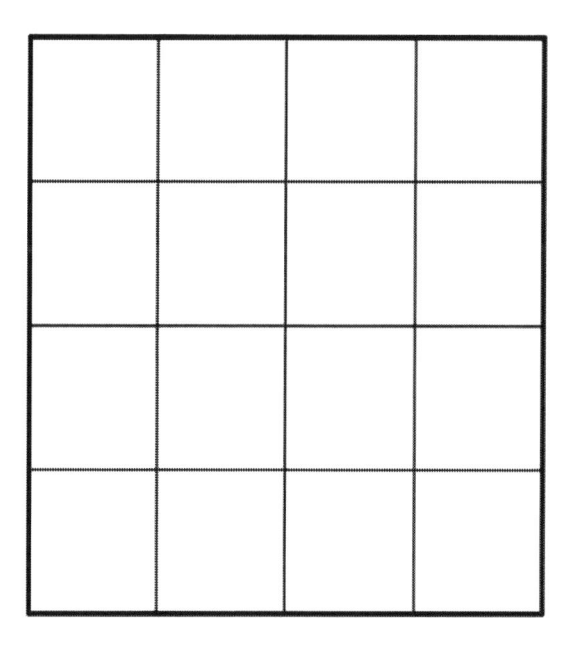

The immediate answer normally given is 16 and I know that for most of you reading this article, 16 is the answer that automatically popped into your head without the need for conscious calculations.

If you slow down and think however, you will see more squares because the outer rim makes one square, as do the middle four squares within the grid.

Each corner of four also makes up another square and the same goes if you start at the top left of the grid, go along three squares, down three, back three and up three.

There are also another four squares if you look at the middle of each rim, i.e. go in one square from the top left and then just go down two, along two, up two and back two.

In all, there are 30 squares within this grid but how many additional squares did I add after the original 16?

Many of you will have answered with 14 because the difference between 16 and 30 is obviously 14 but this is our pre-programmed mind in autopilot again, it stops us from actually thinking because we want answers quickly and it duly delivers, but does it?

I never added any more squares, they were already there to see and all I did was bring them to your conscious awareness, no tricks or magic but just an insight on a different way to think and see things. This mind hack sums up the life of many people who only ever see and use the 16 squares, they may at times utilise more by accident but then quickly go back to their comfort zones of 16.

Changing Mindsets – Changing Results   *www.ReecePye.com*

More often than not, they fail to maximise their full potential by seeing and using the other 14, i.e. the potential that's already there within them, waiting to be used.

I'm sure you've heard the phrase 'Think Outside The Box' and probably more times than you care to remember, maybe you even use it yourself and think this is 'the' correct way to think? This is exactly the kind of conditioned thinking that stops people looking inside the box at times to uncover the potential that is already there.

Many businesses spend inordinate amounts of money looking outside the box (the company) instead of looking inside and making it more effective and profitable by using the full set of resources and potential (their people) that's right in front of their eyes. These bosses don't need more insights, they just need better eyesight and mind hacks help re-train the brain to think differently in this respect. It stops people just repeating phrases like the above without giving genuine thought or applied knowledge to challenge what the masses just repeat like parrots.

IN CONCLUSION

There is often much more potential in you and your current situation than you can immediately see and one way is not always the best way. There are times to think within the box, times to think outside of it and times not to get in the box in the first place so that you're free of any limitations.

As you journey through this playbook, you will begin to untangle and free yourself of limited thinking, you will see things in ways you may never have done before and gain insights into the true power of your mind in ways just as easy as this example demonstrates.

Mind Hack Example Number 2 - There are three sides to every story.

How many times have we heard the saying 'There are always two sides to every story', it's been ingrained in us since childhood hasn't it and how many of us repeat it to our children, family or friends?

Doesn't it set up an automatic competition or conflict between the two parties involved though, i.e. there's your story and mine, which isn't surprising as society has set up this 'either this or that' scenario for all of us to obey; right or wrong, good or bad, high or low, success or failure and nothing in between, except there is and often will be an 'in between' and not just the two extremes.

Coming back to the story or argument, which is what normally entails, most of us will want to be the right one and win the argument won't we? But then, so does the other person so who's going to back down, whose ego is strongest or weakest, who has the power, status, authority… suddenly it can become quite a battle can't it. This is often where insecure bosses lean on their position to enforce their unwritten law, which is 'I'm right because I have more power than you'.

What if we took a different view and suggested **'there are always three sides to every story'** instead of two, namely: yours, the other persons and then the truth, which is somewhere in between and not necessarily in the middle. Would this not open the minds of each person to uncover all the **pertinent facts** to try and arrive at the truth rather than trying to win over the other person because when one person wins, the other person loses and it's not a nice feeling for anyone.

Looking for the truth however, makes the conversation less confrontational and provides the platform (new and different thinking) to ask questions that arrive at the best solutions, the right answers, actions or outcomes. Going into situations like this with more of an open mind rather than it being set as in mindset - you begin to re-train your brain (and the other persons too, hopefully) of being able to turn a situation of conflict into one of collaboration.

"When you change the way you look at things, the things you look at change" Dr. Wayne Dyer

This is essentially what a mind hack does, it opens up and re-trains the mind to a new way of thinking, feeling and acting, which offers a more collaborative approach to how we behave than just going with our 'auto-pilot' reactions. This method of re-thinking has a powerful effect on us over time because it's quick to absorb and often delivered in a question format that makes us challenge ourselves and our conditioning rather than following the herd mentality, the way the masses think!

This raises another question about conditioning because there's a saying that **'Great Minds Think Alike'** but if you truly think about it, they don't actually do they. Some people are great because they think differently, they're creative, innovative, inspiring whereas the masses that think the same are the masses of average people. This isn't a criticism, just an observation.

Regular exposure to these new kind of insights can create quite a collective effect with little or no effort needed to put them into practice, e.g. if a weekly mind hack opens us up to use more of our potential but only improves our personal effectiveness by 1%, then over a period of one year, we could potentially see improvements in excess of 50%!

Ask yourself if you can improve your personal effectiveness or income by 50% this year and you may well balk at the idea but 1%, and then 1%, followed by another and another? What about 5%, then 5%... the compound effect of such growth is powerful indeed.

It's an easy way to make significant improvements and this was the philosophy used by Dave Brailsford, which earned him a Knighthood. It enabled him and his coaching team to turn British Cycling into World & Olympic Champions and they termed the process as 'marginal gains'.

"We are always striving for improvement, for those 1% gains, in absolutely everything we do" Sir David Brailsford

This 'slight edge' is what makes the difference between ultimate winners and those who fall short. Having seen this methodology being used and adopting it with individuals, teams and businesses long before it became popular, I've found it works uncommonly well and has resulted in record breaking sales, industry leading teams, along with establishing market leading high tech firms in the UK and turning around loss making businesses that went on to be sold to market leading brands.

"Success isn't overnight. It's when every day you get a little better than the day before. It all adds up". Dwayne Johnson – The Rock

Using mind hacks to re-train the brain in ways that interface between our inner selves and the outer world is a wonderfully easy and enjoyable voyage in gaining a higher level of self-understanding. When you open your mind to new ways of thinking, you open yourself to new opportunities and will be surprised by how they appear, almost out of nowhere at times, like the 'Law of Accident' but that's for another day.

Free Mind Hack Action Planner Version for the above.

As they say **'Insight without action is worthless'** so for some extra help, you can use the 'FREE' action planner version that goes with the above Mind Hacks, you will find these at the foot of my Mind Hacking page on my website.

CHAPTER 1 - THE SECRET OF TRUE SUCCESS

THE GODS IN THE HEAVENS DISCUSS SUCCESS

Applying the neuroscience of storytelling.

Photo courtesy of Nghia Le

Everyone's looking for something but it's often the case that they're looking in the wrong places, this story shows you where to look.

There's an ancient parable about all the Gods congregating in the Heavens to discuss the fate of mankind because they saw human beings not using anywhere near the full powers they had been given and in some cases, people in high places were abusing their powers.

People were constantly trying to gain advantage over others, abusing their religions, their families and friends. The Gods were seeing a decrease in morals, ethics, feelings and care for others. Humans were ignoring wisdom in favour of possessions and status, the world on Earth was becoming a very selfish (selfie) place to live. Humankind seemed doomed for self-destruction unless something was done about it. Being very concerned, the Gods decided that the wisest thing to do, would be to take away the secrets of success and happiness from those who abused their God Given Powers.

They would take this secret and hide it where very few would ever look or find it, the question was 'where' would they hide it so the few good people deserving of such success and happiness could only find it?

One of the Gods suggested "Let's bury it deep in the earth" but the wisest of the Gods answered, "No, that will not do because it's human nature to search so they will dig into the earth and find it."

Another God said, "Let's sink it in the deepest ocean." But the Wisest God said, "No, not there, for they will learn to dive into the darkest depths of the ocean and will find it."

Then another God said, "Let's take it to the top of the highest mountain and hide it there." But once again, the wisest God replied, "No, that will not do either, because they will eventually climb every mountain and once again, take the secret for themselves."

Changing Mindsets – Changing Results   *www.ReecePye.com*

Then the Gods gave up and said, "We do not know where to hide it, because it seems that there is no place on earth or in the sea that human beings will not eventually reach." They all thought for a long time and then the wisest God said, "Here is what we will do. We will hide the secret deep inside the mind of mankind for them to discover it for themselves. We know from experience that few will ever think to look for it there, these few will be the deserving ones."

All the Gods agreed that this was the perfect hiding place, and the deed was done. And since that time humans have been searching outside themselves, digging, diving, climbing, clambering and exploring – trying to find that magic something that is actually, already within them.

SUCCESS IS NOT WHERE YOU EXPECT IT TO BE FOUND

This parable highlights a fundamental **TRUTH,** that success (True Satisfaction & Happiness) begins in the mind, inside of us first and whatever we become or gain in terms of fame, fortune, material possessions, power or whatever success, ultimately ends in the mind too.

I've seen those (and been one of those at times) who've 'chased the money' without developing a **strong mind**, only to find that the money they desired so much, eluded them or was short-lived. In my experience, developing a **strong Mind** is what enables the financial rewards to 'follow' and not the other way around, money doesn't give people a **strong mind** in the true sense of the meaning although it can give a level of superficial confidence and even, arrogance which are not the same things as a **strong mind**. So the journey to developing and possessing a **strong mind** begins at first by looking on the inside and not externally because it's how we feel about ourselves from the inside and how we express this to the world on the outside that matters to us most of all.

The question then is not so much 'who am I now' but 'who will I become and why' - what's my reason and is it compelling enough to move me mentally and physically towards the person I want to be?

This book is therefore based on Self-Science really and is designed to give you the key elements that form a **strong mind** and it is this inner quality that will help deliver the outer successes.

"Success based on anything other than personal fulfilment is bound to be empty" Dr. Martha Friedman

LEARN EASY – LEARN FAST – LEARN WELL

I wish I'd been taught what I am about to share with you years ago. It has taken me considerable time, money, effort and energy, studying, learning, applying, testing and refining through practice but because I've done this, you won't need to. It's all condensed here within this playbook, in a way that enables you to apply what you learn to your own unique position, situation, environment, personality.... instantly and every day!

You will learn how to hack deep inside your own mind to understand the secrets for your success and happiness, whatever these terms mean to you personally. We will cover the Self-Science of ethical Mind Hacking to bring out the very best in you, for you and for the benefit of those nearest and dearest to you.

I've used Brain Science and Mind Hacks for most of my working life but never knew them by these terms until later in my career, it really does help put a simple but dramatically effective framework around self-discovery and accelerated self-growth.

All issues of humanity come down to one single thing, our inner psychology, how we communicate with ourselves and how we communicate with others, namely the way we and they, think, feel and act, which form our egos, healthy or destructive and anywhere in between.

And, whilst we need the ability to think, it is our feelings, our emotions that drive us, in fact it's emotions and the egos that drive the whole world if we're honest with ourselves.

Emotions are like 'Energy in Motion' that move us mentally. Emotions are more intense than thoughts alone and so the impact of our thoughts are then multiplied, I therefore use a simple equation **EM^2** to signify and simplify what emotions do to us and their impact on others, they effectively create mental **Energy in Motion**, which can be multiplied in

Changing Mindsets – Changing Results   *www.ReecePye.com*

intensity. We'll look in detail at where our emotions come from and how to manage, control and change or improve them for ourselves to reduce the stresses that negative emotions create and increase the beneficial effects of positive ones.

Learn how to master your thoughts and emotions and you will then have the know-how to master and influence those of others, providing you use these secrets ethically, you will get more of the things you want in life by helping other people to get more of things they want in life. Using techniques like mind hacks to re-train the brain, provides an effortless way to learn fast and add vital success principles that can be used to improve the lives of anyone and can change lives instantly, from the moment you let them work for you. This program or guide in a book, is therefore not about me and what I know, it's about you and what you can learn, to become the person you want to be. It combines age-old wisdom and universal truths with the most modern findings of inner success psychology and neuroscience.

Throughout this playbook, I want the content to act as your mentor, giving you the short-cuts to learning easier and faster but balanced with the work you need to do to command the mind you deserve to have and can use for good in your life. Having said this, you'll need to do some work outside of this program yourself, by this I mean education by way of an additional investment in yourself.

HOW YOU CAN GO FROM WANNABE TO EXPERT.

My first introduction to high value professional sales was a rude awakening because I entered to arena with bucket loads of self-belief, only to find that I was totally unprepared for what was to come, through my own ignorance. I'd joined the National Sales Team of a major directory publisher as the youngest account manager by far. "All the existing account managers are old men (they were in their late 30's) who play golf half the week and sleep in the afternoons, I'll show them how to do it" I said to my boss! And then, OUCH! It was a whole new game selling to enterprise level customers compared to small businesses and I learnt in year one that I just wasn't the bees knees after all.

I needed a way to lift my expertise (from virtually nothing) if I was going to be **credible** enough to compete with the peers I now had **respect** for and importantly, win the **trust** and business of major clients. These factors became what I termed the **'3 Step CRT Influence Process', which** I'll cover in more detail later in playbook. I managed to achieve this and was recognised for 'Distinguished Sales Awards' and even a one-off 'Outstanding Contribution to Business Award' too but not without being lifted by my peers. Success came in two ways:

Firstly: I invested time with my peers, shadowing, observing, asking questions and testing their methods with my style. I didn't learn masses but the quality of advice was brilliant and I'm truly thankful and give credit to some of my successes to them.

Secondly: I invested both my own money and time in relevant education over and above anything my peers or company were providing. This included gaining insights into business from world renowned 'thought leaders' across a wide range of business matters. By adding such knowledge, I saw my **credibility** with senior execs increase, **respect** be afforded me for the advice I gave and ultimately **trust** was earned in a way that set me apart from my competitors.

I say this not to brag but to impress upon you, how critical it is to invest in yourself in more ways than just this playbook. And, to continue learning and adding to your knowledge forever more. It's stimulating, it's fun, it helps inspire new ideas, it keeps you growing as a person. I obviously don't know your preferred learning style but for me, it had to be quick, easy and most of all - impactful!!! I wanted information that would make a meaningful contribution to what I did for a living and not just information for information sake.

I researched many options and came across some outstanding ways to **LEARN EASY – LEARN FAST – LEARN WELL** by way of summary books that could be read and digested easily in an evening or weekend and audio books that I could listen to whilst driving or flying, which I did a lot of in those days. I found the following to be invaluable as quick and easy ways to learn:

Soundview Executive Book Summaries www.summary.com because they took the best selling business books published each year and condensed them into just 8 pages typically. So, there's no filler of fluff but just the core messages. Added to this, they have a massive back catalogue of the worlds leading management thinkers. Plus, they've launched a quick-hitting video library of more than 1,000 business tips too, including *BEST IDEA*™ Videos.

To ensure I kept right up to date with current developments and trends in business, I used Harvard Business Reviews www.HBR.ORG because these gave me access to articles not available elsewhere and which, were also like complete books condensed into just a few pages.

I've also referred to compressed non-fiction books via www.getabstract.com because each book summary includes: 1, a rating 2, the top take-aways 3, a full summary 4, significant quotes 5, an author biography and other key points – all of which can be absorbed in less than ten minutes.

In terms of audio, I've used a vast array of providers from direct companies to audio portals like iTunes, Soundcloud and www.audible.com in particular have over 21,000 business books by category, recency, length and language.

In my **'Six-Figure Success Essentials'** framework at the end of this playbook, I include Self-Education as a key element in achieving success beyond what you might think is currently possible. It opens doors and adds to your self-confidence in ways you just wouldn't believe. Adding to your knowledge that others don't have will set you apart, increasing your competence and confidence. So, don't rely solely on your company training because everyone else gets the same training and it therefore won't make you any different to anyone else.

It's a never ending journey of growth and personal accomplishments but most of all, it's an enjoyable and rewarding one if you possess the inner drive to become more of your **True Self** by educating yourself as just one of the ways to develop your **Strong Mind**.

Whatever you learn, try to use it or put it into practice as soon as possible otherwise it just becomes another piece of information stored in your head doing nothing. And make sure the education is not just academic but is practical in nature, e.g. learning from one of my senior peers in national sales was so simple and yet made such an impact on my results that I replaced him as the top performer.

He gave me three key pieces of advice:

1. Get clients to visit Head Office to a) impress them with the quality of processes and b) increase the number of internal contacts that could take pressure off him from an admin point of view. Because when he's done so, he's never

Changing Mindsets – Changing Results   www.ReecePye.com

lost a client and it helped ensure his customer retention was the highest in the company.

2. Take clients to lunch, not as a gift or perk but because when you did this, you get behind their work mask, uncover personal challenges and motivations, and build a stronger, more trusting relationship.

3. Negotiate with your company on the behalf of the customer, rather than the other way round because if you do the best possible deal (within company guidelines of course) for the customer. It ends up being the best deal for the company this way too because the customer gets a better return on their investment (ROI) and is therefore more like to stay as a customer but also increase their spend with you compared with your competition.

Being young and a bit naive (otherwise known as ignorance) I'd considered items 1 and 2 as frilly, fluffy stuff that were more like schmoozing than being professional and businesslike. Once explained to me though, they became part of my modus operandi too. As for item 3, I'd always considered myself a strong negotiator and got the highest price I could from customers but my customer retention was not brilliant, until I applied my colleagues' advice. I'm sure some companies would still balk at the idea of number 3, just as I did before understanding what it could do for me personally, for my company and of course, for my customers. This piece of advice was a sure-fire win-win-win combination. These 3 pieces of advice, added to the investment in my own business education enabled me to break records for customer retention, growth and new business generation all in the same year, which resulted in my first ever 6-figure paycheck. This is in no way meant to sound like I'm bragging but rather, that learning from the top performers (and most are willing to share if you ask nicely) and adding to your own knowledge is a powerful combination to improved performance, higher status in terms of respect from those around you and of course, increases in income too.

Remember: **Leaders are Readers & Learners are Earners!**

"Consider this program as a research project of enormous significance to you because that's exactly what it is, a project in self-science that enables self exploration, self discovery, self knowledge and ultimately, self-understanding".

CHAPTER 2 - PROGRAMMING OF THE HUMAN MIND

UNDERSTANDING WHY WE ARE, WHO WE ARE & WHERE WE ARE TODAY!

Our full potential knows no bounds and yet as humans, our success in life (whatever success uniquely means to us as individuals) is often bound or restricted by **three key truths**:

1. Our conditioning through programming of information and influences of the past, particularly from adults like parents and teachers but also peer groups and social media exposure.
2. Our lack of study or understanding of how we can tap into our immense mental capabilities to release and realise more of our true potential.
3. Believing that this is the mind we've been given and we are who we are, so why try to change it or why bother because changing how our mind works isn't possible.

People rarely ponder on how we've come to be who we are today and where we are in life but the fact is that we're pretty much products of our environments! Simple logic confirms this and delivers the realisation that where we've grown up will largely determine our religious or philosophical beliefs, e.g. in India it's more than likely Hinduism, in Russia the majority are Orthodox Christians, in Italy—Roman Catholic, in USA & UK—Christianity, in Israel—Judaism, in Thailand—Buddhism… and so on. Such upbringings can be so deeply entrenched that people will take drastic actions to protect their beliefs and in some instances, even kill for them. The same goes for our lifestyle, our accents, political beliefs, outlook on life and people, our views about gender, sexual orientation or age, as well of course, our inner values around trust, honesty, compassion and just about every other aspect of our being. In other words, most of the things we think and get emotional about, and also very protective about have been programmed into us.

The key thing here is that we've had little or no 'conscious control' over which of these we have as our religion or philosophy because they were conditioned into our brains and our thinking from an early age.

"By the time we reach adulthood, the experiences we've faced and our reactions to them have shaped our attitudes and personalities to make us what we are today" *Paul J. Meyer*

We haven't shaped ourselves, our environments have and it's this conditioning that obstructs our view of reality.

WE ARE CONDITIONED PEOPLE, PROGRAMMED LIKE COMPUTERS AND ROBOTS (BOTS).

Everything we've experienced and been exposed to is now a projection of who we are: the whole of our inner psychology, which effectively acts like software that runs computers, only it's running our inner computer, our minds and our lives. This is what our habits are formed of, mainly through the force of impact or repetition of the messaging and information we predominantly see and hear every day. For as long as we've been alive, we've followed that which has been passed down or to us by other people, more often than not these have been unsuccessful or average people who being older, we think and assume they know better so we follow their lead.

Well-intentioned as they are or were, this software is running our life and we're running pretty much on autopilot, at an unconscious level, which we'll cover in more detail in the chapters that follow.

The fact is, we haven't created our own original thoughts or emotions, we've simply been receivers like a wireless gadget receiving radio signals. How does this software condition us? It begins from childhood and has tended to be negative in nature, even though it was meant to be positive and protective, e.g.

Don't speak until you're spoken to.

Don't speak out of turn.

Don't do as I do, do as I say.

Don't rock the boat and you'll fit in.
Don't make mistakes.

Do you recognise any of these?

Basically, all these phrases are designed to condition us to conform a) to the standards, expectations, views of the adults telling us or b) to society and the desire to fit in, not to offend or upset anyone else. But it's not just about what we're told, it's what we see too of course, many people talk the talk but don't walk it. Do as I say and not as I do being a typical example, parents who tell you drinking is no good for you and then sit in front of the TV drinking wine or beer because it helps them to wind down after a tough day!

Peer pressure and social acceptance so we fit in is a particular and significant form of conditioning, one that's hard to break out of and embeds the habit of conforming later in life. Many people feel uncomfortable being different through fear of what others 'may' think. This is just crazy isn't it because we all want people to love, respect, admire us for who we are and not who 'they' think we should be.

I was once advised by a wise manager 'Half the people you meet will like you half the time so you may as well be yourself and have those who like you, do so because they see the real you' and it has stuck with me.

It's funny (or not so funny for some) where life takes us isn't it and how we got to be here, wherever here is. If we were to

Changing Mindsets – Changing Results   www.ReecePye.com

play back the recording of how we've become who we are and where we are today, what would we see?

Would we see ourselves as failures, successes or somewhere in between?

Would we be able to say it was a deliberate plan or the 'Law of Accident' in that we've gone with the currents that have brought us here by making the most of surprise opportunities or maybe some form of combination? I've often thought about this because I got into professional sales more by accident than planning and yet became very successful, breaking records for customer retention, growth and also new business, which enabled me to earn a six figure income early in my career. This is not to brag at all because the income was not deliberate or even intentional but accidental too.

I also became a Head of Sales within a FTSE 100 quite by accident, I got a call out of the blue and thought they wanted me for one of the Account Director positions. It was only at the interview, it dawned on me that it was actually for the lead position. I got the job and here again, we set new standards and were singled out for outstanding contribution to business awards. These were not deliberate either but more by way of by-product of how we thought about and behaved in business, the accolades that followed were therefore also accidental.

I became Managing Director of a business services company by accident too really. As sales director, we grew sales so fast that service operations and admin couldn't cope and I was asked by the investors to take over as MD. I declined the offer but three months later, service wasn't improving and I was asked again to take the lead role. I reluctantly accepted but wasn't sure it was my bag. Anyway, we took this loss making company into profitability, repaid the shareholder loans and set the foundation for it to be acquired a larger corporate organisation.

Believe it or not, even this playbook is accidental too. My intention was to create an interactive course and place it on one or more online learning portals so students interested in managing their minds better could find it. Seeing how much content there was though and printing it out to review and edit made me realise I also had the makings of a book here too, hence why you're reading it now.

Whether deliberate or accidental though, how much responsibility and control would we say we've had in bringing us to this point in our lives, could we explain it?

We all like to feel we're in control of ourselves and tell the story of how we planned out our smart goals don't we but how many of us really have, truly? You hear many stories on the Internet of people who've made it big time, they knew exactly what they wanted and just went out and got it, if you believe the hype of course. I'm sure many such stories have been brushed up a bit to create a sense of wonder, sensationalised to create an emotional impact and sell stories, maybe even fabricated or exaggerated stories of how they got there. I've studied many business 'icons' for want of a better word and found that they all started with an idea, as it grew so did they and as they grew, they saw new opportunities and took advantage of them. Success in one area gave them confidence to be successful in another and so on, success tends to perpetuate more success if you have the right morals and ethics about business.

Take Richard Branson for example, can you tell me that when he started off selling records he had a grandiose plan to launch successful businesses in airlines, financial services, health & fitness, hotels, gambling, care services, trains, ballooning and other experiences, telecommunications, broadband and mobile networks... for a start, broadband and mobile weren't even around when he kicked off his first businesses! I also understand that his parents bailed him out when he had a tax issue and if it were not for them, who knows where Sir Richard would be today!

People like this however, are rare indeed and yet aren't these the very people we constantly told to try and emulate? I recall an excerpt from J. Paul Getty's book **'How to be Rich'** where he asks the question about the one thing that will almost guarantee success, his answer was telling, i.e. the current and full use of whatever talents or resources you have available to you. This pretty much sums up the difference between being conditioned and staying this way or making use of what we know or have to begin a new journey of our own making.

These examples demonstrate that we don't need to have our whole lives planned out in detail or try to be the next Richard Branson as some of the 'motivational gurus' would have you think but we can take more control of who we are, how we maximise our capabilities and what impact this has on our levels of success, which can grow and grow. We shouldn't ignore these facts but acknowledge and accept them for what they are, reality up to this point in time and that from now on, we are able to take 'conscious control' of what we allow into our minds by way of influence. You will learn how to pull your own strings rather than you being pulled every which way by your environment and other people.

This playbook is therefore designed to be part of that journey and being better today than you were yesterday and better tomorrow than you are today, it's about progress and progress means growth… in who you are and what you give and get in life.

"You can't change the past but you don't have to repeat it" Elmer Letterman

WE MUST ACKNOWLEDGE THE TRUTH AND USE IT TO TAKE BACK CONTROL OF OUR MINDS!

Because we are conditioned or if you like, pre-programmed by our environments, we find ourselves less open minded and more rigid as we get older and it becomes more and more difficult to alter our character traits or our thinking habits. In effect we've been programmed by everything and everyone we've been exposed to: including Social Media, Books, TV, Radio, Peers, Friends, Family, Bosses, and of course, various celebrities, including the fake reality 'stars'.

To give you an indication of how corporations are trying and succeeding in programming us, especially the youth of today, check out the following content from CBS News, it's frightening! The summary version is just a taster and I'd definitely recommend investing quarter of an hour watching the full version to get the big picture because it doesn't just show the impact on our minds but also the inter-connecting impacts on our bodies.

https://vimeo.com/212594078 (4 min 30 sec)

https://www.youtube.com/watch?v=awAMTQZmvPE (14 min)

Added to this, you have sites like Trip Advisor and Google Maps giving out points and badges for ratings and reviews, which all add to the addiction mentality that is prevailing in society today.

Today, robots are acting more like humans and humans are acting more like robots!

When technology began it was all about humans programming computers and robots (bots) but now the tables are turning and the bots are programming us, much of it by unrealistic comparison to others. We have to ask if Social

Media is going too far in its quest to monetise their offerings versus the original purposes of connecting people worldwide.

Whatever your thoughts, you cannot argue that we're constantly being bombarded with messages, advertising, marketing, news…. It's never ending and often very distracting from who we want to be and what we want to be paying attention to in our lives. Collectively, these run our minds and our lives if we're not consciously aware of it and we risk running around like all the other robotic humans beings, all pretty much the same, all conforming, all trying to fit in. Have you ever had or more to the point, how often have you had an underlying feeling of unease about conforming to the norm and not going against the grain, swimming against the tide, bucking the trends? It's an inner nagging feeling of you not being you but being what's expected of you by society, your environment so you 'fit in'?

You just can't put your finger on why but something is saying to you that everything's not all right, although you're unsure what it is and therefore don't now how to fix it? This is how many people feel their entire lives, right up until their dying days when they look back and say **'I Wish I'd Done This or That or Been This or That'.** It's a dark cloud for many people that follow them around whist they're chasing the ever-elusive dreams that the experts and gurus tell them they should have. Find and follow your passion they say!

Well, some people just don't know what they want in terms of a dream or a passion but they would like life to be better and

Changing Mindsets – Changing Results	www.ReecePye.com

then some, a step at a time rather than following the masses who are marching to a drum that beats to a different tune than the one want to march or dance to. Fighting for your own integrity and being or doing what you want means taking a psychological stand, one that few take responsibility for and Henry Thoreau sums it up well in his famous quote:

" **Most people lead lives of quiet desperation and go to their graves with the music still in them**"

This is where you've separated yourself from the crowds, the victims of circumstances because you're taking action to study, to explore and discover more of your untapped potential. I take my hat off to you for stepping off this treadmill and will do my very best in the following chapters to help you accomplish what you decide to set out for yourself.

At this point, you may well be experiencing mixed feelings and asking 'why haven't I been exposed to these obvious truths before and if they're true why don't more people know about them but this is a part of the programmed you getting in the way. Waking up to this truth is the foundation on which you can build a new you or release the you that is deep inside, the natural, confident, happy you, enjoying life to the full. This may appear selfish in some way because you have feelings of wanting to help and contribute to the lives of others but you must realise this, the stronger you are, the more you can help others, it's that simple. By first being true

Changing Mindsets – Changing Results www.ReecePye.com

to yourself, you will then find that the genuine effect you can have on others will be the most valuable currency there is.

WHAT'S COMING UP NEXT?

The next two chapters will open your mind to new ways of thinking and will also challenge your current conditioned way of looking at things but the great news is that you don't need an MBA or an advanced degree in brain or neuroscience to understand and apply the principles I will uncover in the following pages, you can just start where you are now with what you have!

CHAPTER 3 - THE POWER OF MIND HACKS

BENEFITS OF MIND HACKS

One of the key benefits in developing a **Strong Mind** is to learn how to hack into the depths of your own mind (and not have others doing it through manipulative brain hacking) because by doing this, you will:

- Control the inner workings of your brain for more effective use, which will be covered more in the next chapter.
- Be able to train it to significantly improve and influence your own thinking and emotions far better than you ever thought possible.
- Understand the mind of others so you know how to influence their thinking and emotions far more effectively for the benefit of all concerned.
- Add knowledge through simple Mind Hacks, like the examples and stories you've already been exposed to so far in this playbook to help accelerate your success.

This modern day brain training provides shortcuts to re-program ways of thinking, feeling and behaving so you achieve your personal aims and objectives in life better and faster.

It enables you to be more aware of your thoughts and to manage and use them in more intelligent ways, in effect it's an elevated way of managing and taking control of your mind, which in turn, gives you more control of your life.

WHY ARE MIND HACKS IMPORTANT FOR YOU?

I've always been fascinated by the human mind, the way conscious thoughts and unconscious emotions work together or against someone - what it is that makes the difference between how successful people manage their minds versus those less successful or troubled people, whose minds manage them. I stumbled across the principle of mind hacks during research many years ago and now share this secret method of mind management (secret, because so few know about it) for the benefit of others. Like computer hacking experts, mind hacks enable you to get into your own operating system (your brain) to find and remove bugs that slow the system down or cause it to malfunction. They help fix and improve the software (your thinking) so that it functions well and as it was intended. It enables your mind (the operator or programmer) to manage your brain for maximum results. By understanding how to influence your own mind through mind hacks, you can become a master at getting into and influencing the minds of others too, ethically so of course.

When you think about it, the brain is a fearsomely complex information-processing piece of human technology - one that often eludes our ability to understand it, so we often try not to, accepting instead that this is the brain we've been given and we are who we are, which stops many of us from trying to improve it's functioning.

Just like a computer, most of the software will run in the background automatically once installed properly but it still needs updates and maintenance.

Ensuring the software (our thinking) works to maximum efficiency and making major requirements or requests for change to improve the operating system (our brain) will require your conscious input, commands and re-programming, which I will show you how to do with ease.

MIND HACKS HELP MAKE YOU STRONGER AND SMARTER!

Mind Hacks can change your brain and how smart you operate it instantly - from the moment you begin letting them work for you. It's a powerful method for realising the full potential of your brain and consequently, your full potential in life. Mind hacks often play a pivotal role through **The Neuroscience Of Storytelling** that enables the brain to effortlessly absorb powerful and accurate guidance or insights to make you re-think in ways that make you smarter.

So, mind hacks combine the wisdom of the ages with up to date neuroscience techniques to deliver modern day brain training and shortcuts to re-program ways of thinking, feeling and behaving. They interrupt the pattern of conventional (conditioned) thinking to create new thought patterns, more productive mental states and ultimately, more successful outcomes.

THE POSITIVE IMPACT OF MIND HACKS

Whether you face any of the following situations, mind hacks can help you find the solutions:

- Feeling stuck generally
- Entrepreneurship is proving tougher than you imagined
- Your career or business life has stalled
- You're doing well but want to raise the bar in terms of performance and profits
- You've lost your passion for work
- You're thinking about throwing in the towel

Mind Hacks are for you if you're facing any of the above. The alternative is that you carry on as you are so just remember:

"Old ways won't open new doors" *Anon*

WHERE DID MIND HACKS ORIGINATE?

Let's explore the real facts about Mind Hacks in relation to how it's being applied to computers and technology, namely: improving the operating efficiency and security of systems so that only authorised people can access the systems for the legal intended use.

Hacking is a term popularised by highly skilled computer experts that use their technical knowledge to overcome a problem.

Hackers are individuals who enjoy the intellectual challenge of creatively overcoming limitations to achieve novel and clever outcomes.

They're often seen as mavericks and geniuses that use their creative expertise to circumvent the limitations of a device or system. Today, they're heavily employed by major corporate organisations and governments to legally find vulnerabilities and improve systems security, against cyber crime in particular. To quote one of the most famous hackers of all time; Richard Stallman

"What they had in common was mainly love of excellence and programming. They wanted to make their programs as good as they could be and also, so they could do neat things. They wanted to be able to do something in a more exciting way than anyone believed possible and show "Look how wonderful this is. I bet you didn't believe this could be done."

Using mind hacks to add to your knowledge, the neuroscience of story telling and insightful anecdotes will enable you to achieve this too by training your mind to think and do things in different, more exciting ways and accomplish things that you maybe didn't believe would be possible before reading this playbook.

This may sound complex, a little daunting or even impossible at first thought (that's your old conditioned mind in play) but let me assure you, it's not. There's a proven method for becoming your very own **Mind Hack** expert (maverick or genius) and gaining the benefits that many go their graves never ever exploring, knowing or using.

In Summary

The two mind hacks in the introduction are examples of how they help create changes in how we see things, opening the mind to new, fresh, alternative ways of thinking and you'll be introduced to more examples throughout the book.

In the next chapter you will learn more about brain science so you begin to see how the brain functions and how you can use your mind to hack into and train your brain more effectively, nothing too academic though but just a practical understanding for you to quickly grasp and easily use.

This will enable you to reach the deeper recesses of your mind to:

- Bring negatives to the surface where they can be handled more effectively rather than allowing them to control you unconsciously.
- Recognise the positives inside you so that you can build on and maximise these strengths.
- Become super-conscious and aware of what's going on in and around you so that you become alert, calm, focused and more controlled and in command of who you are and how to act.

CHAPTER 4 - KEY ELEMENTS OF BRAIN SCIENCE FOR MIND CONTROL

UNDERSTANDING THE DIFFERENCE BETWEEN OUR BRAIN AND OUR MIND.

It's important at this stage to understand the differences between our brain and mind so the following points are worth noting. By way of qualification, this is one of the longest sections and is probably the hardest part of the program because we take a 'deep dive' into the brain and its four key components that impact on how you think and feel. It's vital information that when understood, can turn new lights on in your mind, and more brightly... so, make sure you stick with this section, makes notes, re-visit parts to understand it fully.

THE BRAIN AND THE MIND

"Your **brain** is part of the visible, tangible world of the body. Your **mind** is part of the invisible, transcendent world of thought, feeling, attitude, belief and imagination. The **brain** is the physical organ most associated with **mind** and consciousness, but the **mind** is not confined to the **brain**". The intelligence of your mind permeates every cell of your body, not just brain cells. Your mind has tremendous power over all bodily systems, including the heart. **Dr. William B. Salt**

This explanation helps us understand why we often hear sayings like 'the decision was made with the head or the heart' and that the 'brain thinks' whilst the 'heart feels'. The reality is that the heart sends more signals to the brain than the brain sends to the heart but it is the 'mind' that interprets the messages in both cases. Your brain does all the processing but it is the mind that has the ultimate power to manage and make changes to the brain - understanding how the key elements of the brain work is a vital step in taking control.

"Progress is impossible without change and those who cannot change their minds cannot change anything"
George Bernard Shaw

WHAT NEUROSCIENCE IS TELLING US ABOUT OUR BRAIN POWER

In recent years, much has been learnt about the brain and the power of our minds, including how neurons work to effectively 'wire' our brains, the amygdala, which acts as our emotional control centre, the pre-frontal cortex used for conscious thinking or reasoning and much, much more.

The field of neuroscience is a complex one and we're not brain surgeons fixing life limiting brain issues, just normal human beings trying to understand why we are the way we are and how we can make some changes for a better today and tomorrow, right? This section is therefore not designed to be academic but simple enough to cover the core workings of the brain and how, by becoming aware of this, you can use the knowledge to be more effective and efficient in how you use it, rather than it using you.

Armed with this information, the doors of your mind will be opened so you can mentally climb in and make the changes you want, remove the bugs (limiting thinking, invalid beliefs) that slow you down or hold you back and add to or build on your strengths to accelerate your success and lift you to new heights.

So, to make your mind stronger, you will learn how to manage and re-program your brain with the kind of information that makes a positive difference to who you are and who you will become.

THE TECHNOLOGICAL BACKDROP – MIND POWER IN PERSPECTIVE

Let's consider then, the power of the human brain for a few minutes. Digital advances are being made at lightening speed, with voice recognition (VR) and artificial intelligence (AI) applications changing the way technology and humans interact with each other.

We just have to ask Google, Siri or Alexa to pull up the information we want, when we want it, no typing, no fuss - okay, sometimes there's a little confusion but generally speaking, all this without much effort on our part. Added to this we have robots performing previously held human jobs and humans walking around like robots on autopilot on their smart phones and gadgets, so completely occupied that they don't have to think for themselves but just follow the crowd.

Henry Ford was once quoted as saying, **"Thinking is the hardest work there is, which is probably the reason why so few engage in it"** and from experience, I've found this to be true, some people just don't like doing it. If you go about it in the right way however, it can be fun, exciting and most of all rewarding. When you combine brain science knowledge with mind hacking know-how it creates a powerful union, one that shows you the right way to think, the enjoyable life enhancing way.

When you think about it - all these high tech advances and the miraculous tools we have available at our fingertips, have been created by human beings or more precisely, the human mind – the human mind is the 'programmer' creating all other computers and high tech gadgets - how cool is that? I say this because if you actually **STOP & THINK** just for a moment, yes I genuinely want you to **STOP & THINK** right now - the human mind is creating all these new gadgets and tools with that small organ in our heads called the brain, which weighs in just 3 pounds or on average, 2% of our total body weight! Our brains and our minds hold so much power and potential, yet how many people use anywhere near it's full potential, which in turn would enable them to reach more of their full potential in life?

If you search 'how much of our brain power do we use' you'll find listing after listing referring to the myth that we only use 10% of our brainpower! Few of us are that daft (although I know some people who are) and neuroscience research tells us that in fact, we use most of our brain most of the time but here's the crux, we're not using it in the most effective ways, it's all about how we use our mind to utilise our brain power.

With this in mind (no pun intended ☺) IMAGINE what your brain power could do for you as an individual, if you were armed with the knowhow to hack into the immense capability your mind offers, to draw out more of the true potential you possess?

Let's explore the mind (Two Minds) and our brains together in the following pages.

IN TWO MINDS

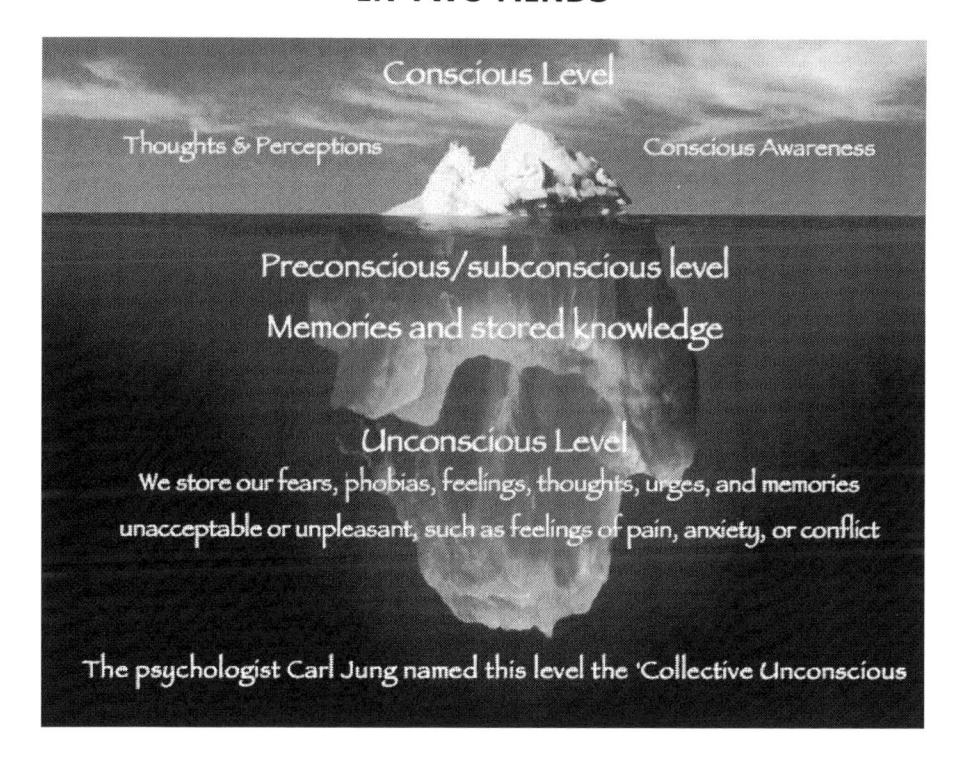

Conscious Level
Thoughts & Perceptions — Conscious Awareness

Preconscious/subconscious level
Memories and stored knowledge

Unconscious Level
We store our fears, phobias, feelings, thoughts, urges, and memories unacceptable or unpleasant, such as feelings of pain, anxiety, or conflict

The psychologist Carl Jung named this level the 'Collective Unconscious'

How often have you said to yourself or heard others say **'I'm in two minds'** because you or they are uncertain about what to do, especially when it involves a choice between two courses of action? Your two minds are effectively in conflict with each other and often it's a battle between 'logic' (conscious) and 'emotion' (unconscious) isn't it?

If you are '**in two minds**' you will find that your unconscious automatically judges whilst the conscious considers, the unconscious reacts whilst the conscious responds.

The unconscious inhabits a world of unexamined 'facts' because that's what's been programmed in from everything and everyone we've been exposed to and influenced by in our lives up to this point, and of course, our own experiences too. This is why we have conflicting values or beliefs and end up confused about what to do at times because it's a fight between our unconscious and conscious minds. We end up acting at times in ways that conflict with how we truly want to be and causing more problems in our lives.

Our brain is a powerful problem solving machine that was meant to provide practical solutions to practical problems but what gets in the way of this however, is that we get emotional and our egos take a hold on us in totally illogical ways, especially our fears, doubts or worries.

They take a stranglehold on us at times so we can't breath, we become hypnotised by the negatives so much that we don't see the positives, the possibilities, the creative sides of our mind get clouded and remain unseen and unused.

The brain and it's pre-programmed thinking has become the master and it loves to be in control - It makes a lousy master however but a brilliant servant, once you know how to manage it properly and take back control.

Let's illustrate this point with a simple question – did you get emotional recently, maybe angry, aggressive, defensive, anxious, resentful, fearful… think back for a minute about how you felt.

Where did these emotions come from?

Did they help you or hinder you?

What was the end result of allowing these emotions to take over your mind?

The reality is that typically, these emotions got you nowhere and only harmed you, made you feel lousy or low, possibly even a little shameful, guilty or depressed. How often does this happen and the other person (it's nearly always another human that stimulated these emotions in you) isn't remotely aware of the impact they've had on the way you feel?

It's even likely at times, that you allowed your emotions to run riot and cause havoc in your life, long after the event, e.g. a conversation, disagreement or argument with someone had passed? In which case, if you continue to carry negative emotions when the other person has already moved on, then who do these emotions harm, yes, you! Not something a clever computer (your brain) or strong mind would consider as an intelligent thing to do wouldn't you say and certainly not something to continue doing?

The obvious next question then, is why do we allow our thoughts and emotions (our internal software) to harm us in this way and how can we alter this to stop the pain and harmful impacts in future?

We must come to recognise that we have to learn ways whereby we can 'hack into our own mind' and take control of the thinking and our deep-rooted emotions in particular, if we are to live the life we want and love the life we have. We must therefore become more consciously aware of the ways in which we think, in order to improve the ways we feel and consequently act, and this is where we can begin to manage our brain much better.

You have a higher level of intelligence that is far more powerful than the brain on its own because you have the ability to use your mind to look in from the outside and notice how you're thinking and feeling. This term in neuroscience is called **Meta-Thinking** or more simply defined as "thinking about thinking", becoming "aware of one's awareness" and higher-order thinking skills. The term comes from the root word Meta, meaning "beyond". If you're interested in a deeper explanation, watch the following video.

Dr. Derek Cabrera
https://www.youtube.com/watch?v=dUqRTWCdXt4

By becoming fully conscious, aware, alert and rational, you are no longer wrapped up in or wrestling with these thoughts or emotions but instead, you can observe, manage and control them in much more constructive and productive ways, and importantly, change them going forward.

Becoming more conscious is important because there are so many things embedded deep within the unconscious mind that we're often unaware of, like subliminal messages and influences that the unconscious has collected and stored for us unwittingly. Then of course, there are also our inherited genes which help form our nature and how often have we heard our parents say 'oh, that's just in their nature' or as parents, we've said the same about our children?

Combine what we've inherited genetically with the repetition and persistence of messages from parents, teachers, bosses, who may state 'you can do this or you can't do this' and which, repeated enough times, you will have formed certain beliefs about yourself and others, unless you consciously disregard them or prove them wrong.

The issue here is threefold:

1. This 'conditioning' is often well intentioned because adults 'think' they know better and when you're young, you're more easily influenced by those in 'authority'.

2. The unconscious mind doesn't think, it just stores everything from the past, it remains in a state of sleep until information stored is required and brought to the surface of your conscious mind at lightening speed and sometimes, with quite intense emotions and feelings.

3. I haven't met the big fella in the sky so can't be sure what he intended when he created us (if you believe in God) but I have a strong inkling that our more intelligent and logical conscious mind was meant to be our command centre. This being the case, how come it's so often overwhelmed and our moods are controlled by the less than useful information

(fears, doubts, confusion, anxiety, anger, aggression, greed, limiting beliefs etc) held within the unconscious?

To quote Eckhart Tolle, the author of **'The Power of Now'** each of these issues can be **'dissolved when we shine the light of conscious thought on them'** and that's a topic we will addresses in the re-programming chapter, educating your conscious mind.

For now, let's explore and understand the other 3 key elements of the brain that impact significantly on our thinking and emotions.

THE AMYGDALA (AND EMOTIONAL HIJACKS)

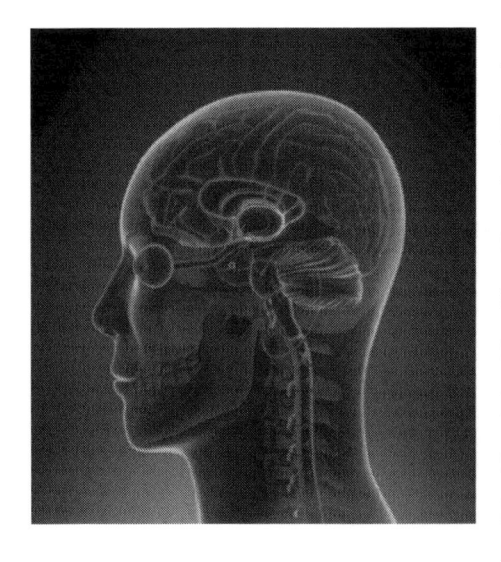

The amygdala is part of the limbic system within the **brain**, which is responsible for emotions, survival instincts, and memory. They act as the bridge between the two minds and I say 'they' because most people think there is just one amygdala but there are in fact two, located either side of the brain, just behind each ear and at the intersection of each eye.

Bearing in mind that we receive most information through sight and sound, the amygdala plays a critical role in controlling how we respond or react to situations and consequently, how we feel on a daily basis. It's like our Sixth Sense, which keeps us aware of all kinds of dangers.

According to neuroscience, the amygdala is the brain's emotional processor commonly associated with fear. They're like the private security guards of our mind in many ways because they raise the alarms to protect us. For real danger (like being chased by a wild beast) this is good but for mental danger, it may not be so. I say this because the fear I'm referring to is anything that conflicts or contradicts with our conditioned way of thinking, and which your brain will perceive as 'danger'. This danger and the associated fear however, is based on our values and beliefs (our programming) held deep within our unconscious mind. This fear reaction can a) stop us from learning something new and b) cause an emotional hijack or as neuroscientists would say, an amygdala hijack that kicks any sense of rational thought or reasoning into touch.

The trauma doesn't stop there in the mind though because the central nucleus of the **amygdala** has direct correlations to the hypothalamus and **brainstem**, which controls the flow of messages between the brain and the rest of the body. It also controls basic body functions such as breathing, swallowing, heart rate, blood pressure, consciousness, and whether one is awake or asleep. In effect, these two small parts of the brain are in charge of all the functions your body needs to stay alive, like breathing air, digesting food, and circulating blood.

The **brain stem** connects the rest of the **brain** to the spinal cord, which runs down your neck and back and if you think about the link with the amygdala, maybe this is where the saying 'they're spineless' came to be recognised because the amygdala raises risk and highlights fear. Just knowing this alone can help open the doors of your mind so you can escort the negatives out and invite new more productive thoughts in. For such small parts of the brain, they have immense power to help or hinder your mental and physical wellbeing.

You cannot bypass or stop the amygdala from working the way they do BUT by being aware of how they work, you have gained a massively helpful Mind Hack that few others will ever understand or be able to use. By becoming more conscious of potential emotional hijacks, which are often perceived and not real danger, you can live in a world of acute awareness that puts you in control of the emotions being sent up through your unconscious and filtered through the amygdala.

I'll share resources and techniques for dealing with negative thoughts and emotions and how to move from such a situation to a more constructive and productive state of mind in a later chapter called **FROM - TO.**

In the meantime, just by knowing and understanding this, you will significantly reduce the number of times you face the

'I'm in two minds' situation. Your mind will be clearer and your decisions wiser and sharper.

For more background information on the amygdala from Joseph Ledoux, a neuroscience expert, just click the link below, his videos are short and very informative. Here's his take on it: https://bigthink.com/videos/the-amygdala-in-5-minutes

SYNAPSES (NEURAL CONNECTIONS) – THE IMPORTANCE IN REPROGRAMMING OR REWIRING THE BRAIN.

You've probably heard the term being used by modern motivational speakers about how the brain is wired and that, to make changes we need to re-wire it. What they're referring to is the fact that the brain is made up of **neural connections or synapses,** a **synapse** is a structure that permits a neuron (or nerve cell) to pass an electrical or chemical signal to another neuron.

To put this into context, each individual neuron can form thousands of links with other neurons, giving a typical brain well over **100 trillion synapses** and up to **1,000 trillion neural connections** by some estimates.

Functionally related neurons connect to each other to form neural networks or otherwise known as wired brains. This is at least 1,000 times the number of stars in our galaxy so it's no wonder our minds are literally all over the place at times.

This sounds complex doesn't it but let me assure you, you don't need to be neuroscientists or brain surgeon to use your mind for what it was intended, to solve practical problems or challenges in practical ways and mind training helps do this considerably well.

What you've learnt already and will add to in the following notes, therefore gives you a distinct advantage over other people who may be familiar with but are not really knowledgeable about the subject of 'wiring' the brain to be more effective, successful, in control and most of all, happy.

Because you will have the ability to understand how your brain works, you will be able to manage and control it better but also, you can (ethically of course) influence others better too.

Currently, your brain is 'wired' in a certain way so you will need to 're-wire' parts of it if you want to make changes in the way you think and feel. Hearing about something is not the same as knowing about something though so it's useful to gain a deeper understanding of the synapses and neural connections.

This part of the section is therefore especially important in your development so let me begin with the 'neuroscience terms' and then I'll summarise them in my own words.

What is the function of the synapse and how do they work in the brain?

The function is to transfer electric activity (information) from one cell to another, the transfer can be from nerve to nerve (neuro-neuro), or nerve to muscle (neuro-myo). When stimulated by an electrical pulse, neurotransmitters of various types are released and cross the cell membrane into the **synaptic** gap (which acts as the junction) between neurons, allowing one neuron to talk to the next neuron and continue sending the impulse across the network of neurons.

These chemicals (which create an emotional reaction or response depending on whether the information is 'perceived' as positive or negative) then bind (wire) to chemical receptors in the dendrites (a short branched extension of a nerve cell) of the receiving neuron. The messages transmitted through the synapses therefore have the power to impact on your mind and your body, and at the same time, e.g. someone says something to you that in effect 'touches a nerve' and not only do you react emotionally but your body follows the lead with a physical reaction such as a headache or tense neck. In this respect, the mind-body connection is one.

My wife suffers from migraines (and no, migraines are not just bad headaches) and tends to get them once tense periods are over, e.g. my daughter competes in dressage championships and at times when she wins, the pressure is released so to speak and the messages in my wife's mind have a physical impact by bringing on the migraine. In this respect, the migraine is not brought on by any negative physical or emotional pressure but a positive mental experience. Many people however, suffer from migraines as a result of the negative emotional pressure and messages transmitting from neuron to neuron through the synapses.

The picture to follow illustrates the process in simple terms but if you'd like more detailed information on the synapses and neurons, I highly recommend the Khan Academy and you can see examples of their content by clicking on their link. https://www.khanacademy.org/science/biology/human-biology/neuron-nervous-system/a/the-synapse

How do neurons "talk" to one another? The action happens at the **synapse**, the point of communication between two neurons or between a neuron and a target cell, like a muscle or a gland. At the synapse, the firing of an action potential in one neuron—the **presynaptic**, or sending, neuron—causes the transmission of a signal to another neuron—the **postsynaptic**, or receiving, neuron—making the postsynaptic neuron either more or less likely to fire its own action potential.

Credit: Khan Academy

In simple terms, my terms.

Synapses are junctions for our internal communications network. The more often you think or feel a certain thing, the more it will open the relevant connection (synapse) and re-enforce it, triggering a chain reaction across the neural network. This is how thinking and emotions can suddenly spiral out of control and cause physical reactions too. So, negatives or positives can be re-enforced and if you want to stop negative thoughts and feelings, you must consciously program positive ones to create new connections rather than trying to change old ones, hence the term re-wiring. In this respect, it's not about changing the information between neurons but making new, more productive connections and repeating them until they become the habits or chain of thinking that you want.

When you consider the number of connections that are repeatedly transmitted through the synaptic gaps over time, you can begin to understand why habits of thought are so difficult to change. Most of these habits of thought or emotional responses are held deep within the unconscious mind, which is why it's so critical to **wake up** and use our conscious mind to make new, more rewarding neural connections.

Compare it to a circuit board where you're in control of the connections, you can disable or unplug those you no longer want or need and create new connections that work for your good.

Photo by John Carlisle

It's with the above in mind that conscious reasoning and decision making from the Pre-Frontal or Cerebral Cortex part of you brain is brought into play, this doesn't mean that all decisions are logical or rational but simply, that you consciously become aware of these two factors in tandem with how you feel, i.e. your current emotional state versus how you want to feel.

YOUR INTERNAL GPS, THE RETICULAR ACTIVATING SYSTEM (RAS) & WYFOYS.

So now you know how to begin re-wiring or re-programming your brain to think in the way you want to more often and less as you don't want. The RAS adds more power to this re-programming through the key senses of sight and sound. In effect it's both a portal through which nearly all information enters the brain but also acts like your own unique internal GPS that guides your attention to what to notice. Although it's already built in to notice things that are important or of interest to you, you can also program it to notice things you want but don't yet have.

So the **RAS** filters the masses of incoming information you're subjected to each day and affects what you pay attention to, how aroused you are, and what is not going to get access to your brain. It's really what the 'Law of Attraction' folks are pushing because they say you attract what you focus on whereas the reality is that you just notice what you focus on more.

You're effectively activating the brain to see opportunities that satisfy your needs and wants. You're not attracting them, you're just noticing them, in a sense (or two key senses actually) keeping your eye and ears open to situations that help you achieve what you want.

Two simple examples are:

1. You're walking through a crowded shopping mall with lots of chatter and noise, and yet out of the crowd, you suddenly 'hear' your name mentioned or called or you 'see' a friend in the distance through lots of other people.

2. You buy a new car and suddenly 'notice' lots of the very same car, even though before you purchased it, there didn't seem to be that many around.

In Summary – Your **RAS** fixes your attention on what you focus on most, if it's negative stuff, you'll notice more negative stuff and if it's positive stuff, you'll notice more positive stuff. This is where **WYFOYS** works and will help you to remember: **W**hat **Y**ou **F**ocus **O**n, **Y**ou **S**ee more of. It's a bit like gardening - you see beautiful things grow based on what you plant in the soil and if you don't plant anything, you'll see nothing. This is where creative conscious imagination can come into valuable play for you and we'll cover this more in the re-programming chapter.

YOUR COLLECTIVE UNCONSCIOUS STOREHOUSE

As mentioned earlier, the deeper mind is the storehouse of all your collected knowledge, your very own library or Google search engine if you like. This can be accessed via the conscious mind, providing you ask the right questions and give it the direction to focus on, namely: what you want and not on the negatives.

To illustrate the power of your unconscious, how often have you tried to think of or remember something consciously and struggled, only for the unconscious to pop it up later when a) it was least expected and b) when you are often relaxed and not heavy in conscious thinking. You made the enquiry through your conscious mind and your unconscious mind delivers as requested, albeit some time later. Thomas Edison deliberately used this method, quote: **"Never go to sleep without a request to your unconscious."**

Another example is when you take familiar travel routes, you've been driving for miles without realising your conscious mind was elsewhere, that is until you came to your turning or junction and suddenly, you woke up mentally. What was it that got you to where you wanted to be, your unconscious mind based on all your stored knowledge and positive habits.

I have friends who commute by train and often fall asleep on the way home (yes, they're overworked and getting old but hey, let's give them a break) but they manage to wake up just before their station.

Again, their mind is working for them when they're not fully conscious. The issue with allowing your unconscious to run your mind (life and business) however, is if you allow it to work in the same way for negative, unproductive and damaging habits, as well as potentially unhelpful or limiting beliefs programmed in from outside influences, it can work against your best interests. This is why shining the light of consciousness on such thoughts and feelings as often as you possibly can, is so important.

This puts you in control of your mind, your thinking, your behaviors. By all means; let your unconscious run your mind when putting on your clothes, brushing your teeth, shaving or putting on your make up but don't allow it to control your key decisions and most important parts of your business and life.

Just remember, unlike your conscious mind, your unconscious mind never sleeps, and is always engaged in figuring out your problems and making key connections, when you use it in a positive and productive way. This is why, many or even most people have their best ideas, solutions, answers when first stirring in the morning, having a shower, enjoying chill-out time or other relaxing pursuits.

So, ask questions and make requests of your unconscious but don't always expect the answers or solutions to be immediate. The unconscious will either draw from the knowledge it has already or because of your request, will focus on outside information **(via the RAS)** to try and bring the answers to you. The alternative to training your brain and controlling your mind is that you continue to try to improve yourself the conventional way, with lots of effort and years of slow learning and little or no progress, continually falling back into old habits like the elastic band that goes back to it's original shape when let go of.

Key Take Aways:

- ❖ When you're awake, be truly awake, alert, aware, notice what's going on in and around you.
- ❖ Use your conscious mind to observe your own thoughts and emotions as an outsider looking in, this way by seeing them, you can manage and control them for your benefit.

- ❖ Ask questions and make requests of your unconscious but don't always expect the answers or solutions to be immediate.
- ❖ If you observe your outer world, I mean really observe the world around you, you will see how most people are going through life like robots (moving computers) in auto-pilot and lost in-thought (unconscious) not really noticing what's going on inside their brains.

They're being driven to distraction, literally, because they're not consciously aware of the two minds and the amygdala effect, the impact of synapses and the connection through the brain stem to the body or, how to use the inbuilt RAS to see and hear more opportunities that align to their wants and needs. Consequently, their minds continue to control and direct them, right up until they're too old to do anything about it.

If you're honest with yourself, how often do you check your phone for messages, social media posts, emails etc and can you say that you're not in any way addicted to technology or having your attention drawn away from what's most important in your life?

I think if attention was money, we'd all be wasting lots of it, basically throwing money away with our attention and all the distractions, in many instances technology is controlling us when we should be controlling technology.

Essentially, many people are asleep, sleep-walking through life, not really awake to what's happening in their own minds and yet, they have a continual nagging feeling that something isn't quite right. This is their real self, their unconditioned natural self, screaming 'SET ME FREE' I want to come out!

Whilst you on the other hand, are one of the few who see life in all it's real beauty, consciously aware of how you manage yourself and the positive impact this has on those closest to you and who you come in contact with that can help you achieve whatever it is you desire.

To Wrap Up This Chapter

Understanding the key workings of the brain and how easily mind hacks can open the mind to new truths has made a massive difference to me and it can for you too but please don't just take my word for it, read, consider, really study and think about what you find within this playbook and importantly, apply it, test it, stick with it and prove it's value for yourself.

What's next?

In the next chapter and with the mind hacks and brain science knowledge as your foundation, we will begin the process of self-assessment and positive change.

CHAPTER 5 - WHO ARE YOU - WHERE ARE YOU?

WHO YOU ARE & WHERE YOU ARE RIGHT NOW?

By this point in the playbook, you will already have started to re-program your mind, the way you think, some of the subsequent emotions that come from these thoughts and of course, ultimately how you feel and behave.

Before we can delve deeper into the process of re-programming your mind, we need to understand who you are and where you are right now, not in terms of how you've been programmed but deeper into your nature as a person, who are you really and who is the person you want to let out or become.

I can't recall where I heard the following quote and it may be a bit strong but it does demonstrate the potency of desire that's strong enough to move someone from who and where they are to who and where they want to be.

'I was willing to completely die to any form of me that I have been so that I could birth the person I was to become' Anon

We therefore need a deeper dive inside our own heads to understand why we are, who we are today as the foundation to build the person we can become. And, the reason why a lot of people won't become who they want is because they're still too attached to who they've been and who they are currently. This is not an excuse to become self-obsessed or overly introspective, this is not counseling or therapy but a program to help you build on strengths, eliminate unwanted weaknesses or character traits and become more of who you want to be, now and in the future. Now is the time to begin making some decisions because this is the time you can do something about it, not some time way off in the distance that may never be reached or when you get there, it turns out to be different to what you expected or wanted.

Tomorrow is tomorrow, so our focus will be on the current situation before we move onto re-programming towards the desired situations. This may be, although it doesn't have to be, a little uncomfortable because you'll be looking much more specifically at what's shaped you as an individual, the firmly held values, beliefs and principles by which you conduct yourself today. Challenging your current views about yourself can be a scary thing and potentially changing or updating your values can be especially difficult because they've been so ingrained in you for so long.

And yet, the journey of self-exploration and discovery can also be a wonderfully rewarding activity so let's begin the self-assessment of **W**ho **A**re **Y**ou and **W**here **A**re **Y**ou right now.

I use the mnemonic **'WAY'** because the content within this and the following chapters will help show you the 'way' forward from who and where you are now and who you can become and where you can go.

It will help you answer many questions, including but not exclusively:
- What's my life all about, where's the meaning for me personally?
- What's my true passion, purpose or vocation in life?
- How can I achieve more, easier, faster, better than my current ways?
- Why do I try to be what others expect rather than being my true self?
- I'm capable so why is it so hard to realise my full-untapped potential?
- Why are so many people difficult to deal with, e.g. bosses, co-workers, customers, family, friends?
- How can I take more control of my direction and life in general?
- Why do I have such a hard time focusing my attention?
- How can I clear my mind of excessive thinking and switch off more?
- What can I do to stop my emotions hijacking my moods?
- How can I enjoy life more now and worry less about the future?

- How can I stop being torn between one frantic desire and the next?
- Why do worry, doubts and fear dominate my mind?

The following sections will help you understand what you stand for now and what you intend to stand for in future, it will give you more clarity than maybe you've ever had. Many people will have thought about their values from time to time but we will look at them in a detailed way that will give you a new perspective on how they drive your behaviour.

WHAT DO YOU STAND FOR – YOUR CORE VALUE SYSTEM

Even the most optimistic, enthusiastic and positive people on the planet can feel hampered without crystal clear values and in the absence of such clarity, can easily fall into the trap of losing sight of what's truly most important in their lives. Values are, after all, the things you value most in life. Some people think they know all about values because the subject is touched on in just about every personal development book, course or program that's worth anything. I've not come across any material however, that explain and cover them in the detail that enables people to fully utilise the power they have to move them forward or in fact, hold them back.

In this chapter, you will look at your values in a ways that you may never have done before and will open your mind to why they can be an asset or liability, and often at the same time, which is why people get confused or hesitant. You know your values drive your behaviours and these are not just the things that are important in your life but crucially, your own judgement of what is important in your life. It's a judgement call that requires you challenge yourself and your programming (passed down values) of the past. And here's a truth about your values that may surprise or even shock you – your values can also be the foundation of your biggest fears, i.e. some positive values have a counter value of a more conflicting nature. It's like being pulled back and forth mentally and not really understanding why, this is the reason some people hesitate to act or procrastinate on a particular decision or task.

CONFLICTING VALUES

As well as being in 'Two Minds' in terms of conscious versus the unconscious, there will also be times (frequently for some) when you'll have values pulling you in two different directions and not always either good or bad but good versus an alternative good, which makes decisions even tougher, e.g. as follows:

1. You want to give full commitment to work (value work ethics) and earn as much as money as possible (value the lifestyle it brings) but also want to spend more time with your family (value loving quality relationships).

2. You want to start your own business and become and successful entrepreneur (value independence) but you don't want to give up the income and benefits you're getting in full-time employment (value security).

3. You like being in a relationship (value being loved, cared for) but won't leave the current one, even though it's not working and unlikely to work because you fear the unknown or being alone (value certainty or safety).

4. You want to be seen as a great presenter or public speaker (value being liked, respected or admired) but fear being criticised or looking stupid (value being competent).

In each case, it can become a trade-off between one value and another or a compromise of some kind. What's useful in these situations is to put your values in priority order for each category and then look at each in relation to short, mid and longer-term advantages or disadvantages. This will help make decisions easier and also enable you to explain them more clearly to loved ones or bosses even, if the need arises.

"When your highest values are in priority order, your direction is clear and your decisions therefore become easier to make"

I'll guarantee you this, very few people anywhere will have done this exercise or understood why they have inner confusion based on inner conflicting values rooted deep in the unconscious mind. Some do this is retrospect and deeply regret not doing it in advance of making certain decisions, like one of the three investors I ran a business for from 1997-2000. He was previously a CEO of a retail organisation and made multi-millions from when it was sold off. I recall a time when we were out walking and talking at his farm and his Son passed by on a quad-bike, without stopping, looking over or saying a single word.

What the investor said next was telling and went something like this:

"Do you know something? Having all this money is great but it's only now, looking back that I see what I've missed. I don't have a bond with my kids because I was never around or close to them. I chased the money and got it but lost something that I can't replace, the time and love of my kids when they needed it most".

I've been very fortunate in this respect because not having a Father around made me aware of the impact it can have on kids and so I made sure that whatever job I took or business I ran, it would not stop me from being there for my children and to support my wife.

At the end of this section and in using the templates that follow, you will know how to bring your values to the surface and deal with them in a pre-determined conscious manner, calmly, practically, effectively.

A point of note regarding conflicts with other people.

Conflicting values aren't just restricted to your own mind because they can also spill over into frustration with other people. Like yours, the values or beliefs in fact, of others are voiced as opinions and if they differ considerably with ours, it can be a recipe for conflict. Just by knowing this deeper knowledge however, can enable you to ask more relevant, insightful or challenging questions that lead the conversation down the road that helps achieve the right outcome for all concerned rather than getting into a battle of who's right, just as per the example of 'Two sides to every story' in the introduction. This fact can help you understand and influence others more effectively and collaboratively.

If you're feeling undervalued or unappreciated at work because your values are not being met, whether it be bosses or colleagues, and you're thinking about how to step off the treadmill, the following article with 6 tips may help put your mind in a better place to deal with it without sacrificing your values. https://reecepye.com/blog/f/feeling-undervalued-or-unappreciated-at-work

ASSESSING YOUR VALUES

As mentioned, your behaviours are driven by your inner values more than anything else so make sure they align with who you want to be and not necessarily who you are today, and especially not what you think others expect you to be. You must be true to yourself.

"You can waste a whole lifetime,
trying to be,
what you think is expected of you,
but you'll never be free"
Chris Rea, lyrics from Gone Fishing

Where many people go wrong when looking at their values is they just bundle them up into one long list instead of considering all areas of their life, like relationships, career & financial, family & social, physical & mental, ethical & moral areas. Being clear about them will help make decisions easier for you and avoid unnecessary internal conflict or confusion, which keeps you 'In two minds' about what to do. Doing this exercise will ensure you know your own mind because you'll be working from one strong set of values.

"Values are like fingerprints, nobody's are the same but you leave them everywhere you go and all over everything you touch and do" Elvis Presley

No-one else can dictate what values you decide on for yourself but by way of example, the following considerations should help stimulate ideas and remember, values are the things that are most important **to you!** These form the principles or standards you've lived by up to this point but assessing and deciding on the values that you and not others expect of you, are what will form the principles and standards of behaviour you decide to live by from this point on. Re-asses your values as time goes by because what serves you well now may not serve you well in future. Use your on-going experiences and the facts of each experience to help you decide what values suit you.

Changing Mindsets – Changing Results www.ReecePye.com

Your core natural self will probably not change much and neither will your core values, e.g. honesty in all relationships, give to contribute and not just to get but others can be tweaked or changed at different stages of your life, most notably in relation to career as you rise up the ranks, start to come down or decide to or are forced to change direction entirely.

Relationships: At the end of the day and most likely on your very last day on this planet, all the material possessions you have will make no difference to you at this point in time, it will only be your memories and in particular, those memories that involve loved ones that will matter to you.

Career & Financial: The kind of work that excites or satisfies you most. Your salary requirements. Your training & development. The kind of people you want to work with. How you will spend or invest your money. The things you can acquire and enjoy.

Family & Social: The kind of parent, sibling, partner, friend you want to be. How you want your marriage to be. When and what amount of time you will spend with family and friends. How you will mentor your children to become strong, independent adults. Recreation and holiday activities.

Changing Mindsets – Changing Results

Physical & Mental: How you exercise and how often. The food you eat and when. The books you read and learn from or to help you relax. The habits that link mind and body together. How you manage stress and pressure. Your weight and how you look. Your energy levels.

Ethical & Moral: How you use your time or money to help others. Your integrity. The kind of person you want to be for others. Your religious beliefs and commitment to worship. Local versus global causes. Use of alcohol or drug use (prescriptive of otherwise).

The Hammock Test

This idea was explained to me for someone in old age looking back on life but this doesn't have to be the case, you can choose any age you want and could do it from where you are right now if you like. Imagine you're swinging back and forth in a hammock, looking back on all areas of your life.

What are the things, the experiences, the accomplishments that make you look back with enjoyment and pride?

It's quite an eye opener because it tends to put the different aspects of your life into proper perspective in terms of their real value to you. When you consider all the areas of your life (the above are just my examples) it becomes clear that if one area is 'WAY' out of sync or out of balance with others, it can make life seem unstable, a bit rocky even.

The 'Wheel of Life' methodology has been around for thousands of years and even so, only those few enlightened people use it today to help keep balance in their life. The following excerpt and article by William Anderson, LMHC published on Medium - Thrive Global gives a good summary of the various versions.

Centred and Whole

The purpose of the wheel of life exercise is to make sure our wheel, the whole of our life, is balanced, all aspects or needs fulfilled in the right way. When one aspect of your life becomes an excessive focus and the others are neglected, the wheel is out of balance. We know what happens to an out-of-balance wheel. It gets wobbly and is likely to crash.

How the Wheel of Life Can Help You Find Balance

Within each area of life, the range of possible values and questions to open up values could cover another playbook altogether and will vary widely from person to person, and for different stages of life. The templates on the following pages are generic and therefore by way of example to give you an idea with which to build your own unique versions. They begin with a typical Career type example and then I use two that are very important to me, namely: physical health and family.

THE PASSION PARADOX

Whilst we're on the subject of values, let's take a quick look at them in relation to passion. Everywhere you look today, the 'motivational gurus' are telling you to follow your passion, as if we all have but one single overriding passion and you can suddenly hold it in your hands like a crystal ball and everything you wish or hope for will come your way, just like magic because you've found your passion in life. Right, if only it was that simple!

The business world tells you that the people who make it are passionate, interviewers ask you what you're passionate about as if there is this one 'silver bullet' but it's all just societal conditioning that the masses follow.

The reality is that most people do not have 'a passion' but are passionate about many things, which add up to create what we do well. Our values offer vital clues as to what we're passionate about and it doesn't have to be a particular vocation in life but the process of what we do in our work.

For over 20 years I worked in the directory advertising industry and for much part, I loved it and was very successful, breaking customer retention and new business sales records as an Account Director and setting new standards as a senior exec in a FTSE 100. Was I passionate about directories, absolutely not but I did know they gave value to our clients and giving value was something I was and still am passionate about for sure. It was my passion for excellence (one of my core work values) in everything I did that lifted my teams and me to higher levels of success. I wanted us all to be the best we could be and so studied, applied, tested, corrected and worked at being the best I could be. The results followed as a consequence of satisfying this value and not the other way around.

Another place to begin understanding your highest values and passions is to reflect back on what has made you proud. By this I don't mean self-aggrandising in the sense of your own importance or power but in terms of what gave you a high level of personal satisfaction, whatever you did stood out or still stands out in your life as a special. For example: I'm proud of educating myself and learning to lead a successful team that broke sales records, not because it made 'me' look good (in fact I shy away from such recognition) but because I saw others lift their performances, grow and achieve record breaking results and enjoy good lives at work. The pride came from what we achieved collectively and I just played my part.

As well as looking back to remind yourself of the things that made you proud, you can also project it forward or in fact, bring it right here into the present by asking yourself what sort of things would make you proud to do or accomplish, not just for yourself but the positive impact on those around you too. Pride is not all bad, thinking it is, is just another conditioned and limiting attitude that society bestows on us, i.e. reference to pride being one of the 7 deadly sins.

As with most things in life, it depends on how we view things and apply them so we should not just accept what others have been telling us is the way to think for years.

If you want to develop some passion in your life, check out https://www.youtube.com/watch?v=IXexl8SX8qI by Tom Bilyeu – Founder of Impact Theory for some helpful insights into building your passion.

CORE BELIEFS

The degree to which you start and move towards your desired end results will largely be determined by your beliefs (and confidence because the line between belief and confidence is often a very close one) and whether they are uplifting and empowering or weak and limiting. You may value a particular thing you want to do or accomplish, like starting your own business and becoming a successful entrepreneur (value independence) but you don't believe it's possible?

It should not be a case of 'you either believe or don't believe' though because belief can be built through investigation and acquiring knowledge which adds to the belief (and confidence) that something is possible, i.e. knowledge is power or to be more precise, knowledge is potential power that when acted on, becomes powerful. In the above example, just beginning research about how to start a business, how to run one, who's done it before, successful case histories or stories etc can begin to build belief and as each piece of research is complete the belief and confidence will increase a step at a time to grow stronger. If the desire to satisfy the value is strong enough, the individual will act on the information acquired. Just through some of the research, it could not only begin to increase your belief but you could find it actually inspires you, which is even stronger still and when added to belief, you really begin to see the potential ahead.

I'm not going to dwell on the subject of beliefs to be honest because once you've done the values assessment and prioritised them, the strength of your values and how important they really are to you will drive the desired behaviour to overcome any limiting beliefs or lack of confidence.

You must remember that beliefs are exactly that, just beliefs and in themselves don't make something true or false or anywhere in between, they're 'made up' by ourselves or through programming of the past influences in our lives. As the dictionary explains a belief is 'an acceptance that something exists or is true, especially one without proof' so deal with reality, the facts and focus on satisfying your values. When you do this, you won't need belief as you'll 'just do it' as Nike say in their famous advertising slogan.

Just because you believe in aliens, karma or God doesn't make any of them true and just because you don't believe in any of them doesn't make them false... beliefs are 'your' decisions. This isn't something that people often accept (believe) easily because they've been conditioned for so long. To help shift any existing limiting beliefs however, I show a method for moving to more liberating beliefs (positive emotional states) in the FROM-TO section later in the playbook, which allows you to play around with different templates or create your own to suit your situation.

SELF-MOTIVATION & HOW TO CREATE IT.

Firstly we must understand that every human being is a motivated individual, it's just that some are motivated to do as little as possible, some by what is comfortable and safe, which means staying as they are and accepting their lot in life as it is, others are motivated to be more of the person they are capable of and to experience life to the full.

Some are motivated by fear and do nothing, others are motivated by growth and accept risk or setbacks as exactly that, not failure but just setbacks. So the important question is not 'are you motivated' but rather 'are your motivations good for you' and will they steer and help you move in the direction you want to in life?

In this respect, your values, level of belief and motivation are intrinsically linked.

So what is motivation?

The clearest explanation of motivation I've ever heard and which, I've pro-actively applied in my career to accomplish some (if I may say) pretty impressive successes is this:

MOTIVATION can be summed up in two words, **MOTIVE & ACTION,** in other words a motive or reason to act, the more compelling the reason, the more compelling the actions and the more likely you will follow through to accomplish 'your' desired result and satisfy your values. In the same token, the weaker the motives, the weaker your actions are likely to be.

Like your values, motivation can pull you in opposite directions if you're not aware of how it works, i.e. the stronger the fear and doubt about your ability to achieve what you set out, the stronger the hold on you to do nothing and stay safe in your comfort zone. The stronger your motivation is to achieve what you set out to and the more important the value is to you, the more likely you are to do something about it.

In essence, it's nearly always a trade-off, what are you willing to let go of, e.g. fear, doubt, comfort in order to free up space for the constructive stuff like courage, confidence, growth. With this in mind, it's critical to understand that self-motivation based on your very own and unique inner values as opposed to external motivation from others, is the strongest of all motivational forces because:

a) The motive or reason to act is pre-determined by you.

b) It has more meaning to you personally because the drivers will be your values alone.

c) It will not just be about tangible things like money that drives your self-motivation but also intangible things like becoming a subject matter expert in your chosen field.

d) You can continually find your own reasons to act and don't have to rely on others to motivate you or in fact, demotivate you.

e) It's permanently available for you to call on and apply.

f) It puts you in control of your own motivation.

g) Ultimately, you have the ability to create self-motivation at will.

There are three particular points of note with the above:

1. The reasons to create strong self-motivation are yours and not those of others. If you rely on others to motivate you, e.g. through fear or rewards, then you are handing over control to them. This also results in them being able to de-motivate you. When you develop **self-motivation** however, it is you who is in control.

2. Self-motivation (your motive for action) on it's own is a start but you have to act on this if you are to achieve anything worthwhile, in effect: the motive is the ignition key and action is the fuel.

"If you're working on something that's exciting, that you really care about, you don't have to be pushed. The vision (self-motivation) pulls you" *Steve Jobs*

3. Although unlikely, even after doing the values assessments in the next section, it's possible that you won't find 'compelling' reasons that automatically move you but if this is the case don't worry. You will have some areas to work towards and these combined should get you into action mode so start with these. As you begin to see results, you'll build momentum and as you build momentum, you'll build even stronger motivation. It means having the desire and discipline to at least begin the journey. Oprah Winfrey summed it up well in one her best known quotes: **"Do what you have to do until you can do what you want to do."**

In the next section, we'll look at how and why it's essential to challenge some of your values, beliefs, motivations and we'll cover methods for altering attitudes and behaviours that will help you be who you want to be and achieve what you want to achieve.

IN SUMMARY

You can now take conscious control of what motivates you from the inside and not rely on external motivations (people) to lift you up or pull you down.

You'll find you exude more confidence and self-assurance because you know clearly, what's most important to you in each area of your life, how they fit together for collective impact and where you're heading.

Self-motivation through the inner clarity about what's most important to you and how to avoid inner conflict is a fascinating thing, and in the right hands, can be an absolute superpower once you acquire it because you'll be able to pass it on to others too.

"I understand myself only after I have examined myself and only in the process of understanding who I am now, can I decide who I will become"

WHO ARE YOU - WHERE ARE YOU (WAY) SELF-ASSESSMENTS

TEMPLATE INTRODUCTION

In this section, there are three types of value assessment by way of example that you'll be able to use, amend or create your own. An important thing to bear in mind here is that you should be creative, try new versions, don't be afraid of doing an assessment and not being happy with the first cut, tweak it, change it, add to or remove from it but don't be afraid to make mistakes.

Few things in life are perfect and especially where thoughts and emotions are concerned so understand that this will be an ongoing process of reviewing and refining.

"Perfection is not attainable, but if we chase perfection we can catch excellence" *Vince Lombardi*

TEMPLATE 1 - CAREER & FINANCIAL

The following template is a simple list form, which is broken down into various categories. Here, you just need to rate each one from 1 – 10, with 1 being the lowest and 10 being the highest.

Values　　　　　　**Importance 1- 10 (10 being highest)**

Environment

Casual, Relaxed Work Environment

Exposure to Nature

Fast Pace

High Level of Interaction with People

Location

Physical Activity

Working Alone

Working Outside

Travel

Supportive Management

Growth

Adventure

Challenge

Changing the World

Creating New Things

Intellectually Demanding Work

Opportunity for Advancement

Opportunity to Lead

Opportunity to Learn New Things

People

Camaraderie

Collaborating with Others

Changing Mindsets – Changing Results　　　　　　　　　www.ReecePye.com

Competition

Diversity

Helping Others

Influencing Others

Socialisation

Two-Way Contribution or Sharing Ideas

Fun

Creativity

Laughter

Innovating

Problem Solving

Rewards

Employee Benefits

High Income

Income Based on Productivity

Job Security

Moral, Ethical, Spiritual Satisfaction

Power

Prestige, Status as an Expert

Recognition

Time Freedom

Limited Stress

Work Life Balance

Type of Work

Services

Building Things

Risk Taking

Routine Work

Variety of Tasks

Whilst this list looks long, it could easily be longer still as the criteria for what satisfies your career or work values can have knock-on effects on other parts of your life too so it's critical to cover all values you have in this area of your life.

Add, remove or change any of the above so they're specifically relevant to you and then once you've rated each one, pull all the 10's, 9's, 8's into separate lists.

By grouping them together like this, your list of priorities (career requirements) will become clearer to you and it will be obvious to see where they're not being met right now and importantly, what you need to focus on changing so they're satisfied going forward. For example: Let's suppose that within your ratings, you marked an item in each category as a 10 like so:

Environment - High Level of Interaction with People

Growth - Changing the World

People - Diversity

Fun - Problem Solving

Rewards - Moral, Ethical, Spiritual Satisfaction

Type of Work - Variety of Tasks

Changing Mindsets – Changing Results

Currently you're working in a high pressure environment that offers challenge, competition, innovation, high income, with routine work and you can't quite understand why you're not feeling satisfied... the list of values above might now suggest you work instead in non-profit or charitable sector, i.e. patterns like this give clues to the type of careers or direction you can take.

TEMPLATE 2 - FAMILY

This template is based on a family man with children and is in question form but more by way of challenging you so that you can still use the same 1 – 10 rating methodology. This time however, the rating will be 1 for Strongly Disagree and 10 for Strongly Agree, with 5 being neither Agree or Disagree (which usually means indifference) or anywhere in between of course.

Values   **Questions Rate 1 - 10**

- My family is of significant importance to me and my behaviours demonstrate this to my family.
- I spend as much time with them as is necessary.
- I make time to accommodate special family events.
- My children look forward to seeing me after work.
- I reserve special group and one-to-one time for my children and my spouse.

- My children love and respect me, even if they're being disciplined.
- My family values my opinion and judgment on things.
- I give all members of my family my undivided attention when with them.
- I am genuinely interested in what my children and family have to say.
- I don't bring work related frustrations or stresses home to my family.
- I educate my children in life and not just academics or theory.
- I offer objective advice or opinions to help my children arrive at their own decisions and become independent rather than reliant on me.
- I give genuine praise to my children and build their inner confidence.
- I teach my children discipline and positive work ethic.
- I recognise and respect the differences in all my family members.
- My family adheres to fairness and open-mindedness in dealings with all people, regardless of race, creed or colour.
- All family members have the opportunity to lead in their own way in the household when necessary and not by any controlling demands from me or any other member.

- My family is free to express their views without fear and to make their unique contributions to family decision making when required.
- I express my love and care for my family in both words and behaviours, I willingly show affection to any and all members.
- My spouse and I share common values, morals and ethics.
- Family arguments are few and far between and resolved collaboratively.
- I show tolerance, patience, kindness and compassion in appropriate situations.
- I keep in touch with my wider extended family.

Again, this list may look long but could be longer still, in a nutshell; family is the most important area in the lives of most people so it needs to be given thorough consideration.

Unlike the previous career values assessment where you group ratings in the highest order, here you will be interested to see where the ratings are high (agree) or low (disagree). This will highlight your strongest values but also, if ratings are low and you must be totally honest with yourself here, you will have some work to do. This self-assessment shows you where that work will need to be aimed at. You can of course, build a different set of questions if you're single or in a relationship but don't have children.

TEMPLATE 3 - PHYSICAL

This template is in question form but with assumed values (you need to select your own but using this as a guideline) and simple Yes / No answers. This time however, a 'Yes' will be viewed as a positive and an area that is strong or could be built on further and a 'No' is where there's room for improvement.

Value   **Assumptions: Agree Yes / No**

- I take my physical health very seriously.
- I look and feel good.
- My weight is about right in terms of where I want it to be.
- My muscle strength and muscle mass (which helps burn calories and fat) is adequate.
- My physical activities are good for my health & well-being.
- My work habits do not negatively affect my physical health.
- I make time to feed my body with a healthy, well balanced diet and eat at regular intervals.
- I limit things like alcohol, tobacco, sugar, fats, caffeine intake.
- I recognise excessive physical pressures and head them off early to avoid illness.

- Work absences have been minor or non-existent in the last year.
- I understand and avoid the impact of mental stresses on my physical health.
- My energy levels are always more than adequate to conduct my work well.
- My energy levels are always more than adequate to partake in family activities.
- I make sure to include 'downtime' to re-charge by physical batteries.
- I plan and immerse myself in enjoyable activities for rest, relaxation or recreation.
- I participate in exercise such as walking or running or other sporting activities.
- I get as much exercise as I need.
- I rarely have to take time off work because of physical illness.
- My vacations allow me to unwind and enjoy time with friends or family.

I've only covered Physical Health & Well-Being in this template but you can create a separate one for Mental Health & Well-Being or combine the two and call it Mind-Body for example.

In Summary

As you can see from just the three different examples above, there are many ways you can assess your values and my experience is that most people just bung all values together in one single list (if they do it at all and many don't) only to find the exercise confusing.

When you separate each area of life however, the outcome allows you to see where your highest values become your highest priorities in each area but also, where they impact on each other or in fact, conflict with one another.

In the case where values and priorities clash, it usually means a trade off of one for another but not for ever, e.g. a short-term sacrifice in terms of time with family over a key project at work (for promotion) may well provide longer term benefits in terms of future family time. You can use the following formula to remember the process for reviewing your values.

Q.A.K.A. – Question, Assess, Knowledge, Action.

There's no one answer for all of course but the quality of **Questions** and seriousness of the **Assessment** does help give you quality **Knowledge** about yourself that when combined, gives you the bigger answer with which to **Act** on.

YOUR SELF IMAGE

By conducting the above exercises, you are effectively creating a reflection of who you think you are and what the outside world sees, your values, beliefs, principles are the picture you hold of yourself. And, this is why doing the self-assessments is so critical for you, i.e. you are deciding who you are and who or what you will become. It puts you in control rather than trying to live by the images that society portrays are the right way to be.

We live in a media driven world where we're exposed to or even bombarded with message and images of what's good, e.g. drive this car, wear this make up or these clothes, use this smartphone, go on vacation to these places…. follow the trends, which essentials means 'buy what we're selling or more to the point telling' you. It gives the impression that how we look to the outside world is more important than how we feel on the inside and this is simply not true.

You've probably seen it yourself at times, people with over-inflated images of themselves based on material possessions and comparison with the circles they move in.

Knowing and living by your values gives you the real advantage because you're able to be true to who you are, based on a healthy self-image and self-respect that takes you where 'you' want to go. If your self-image is strong, you will be strong and so will your actions be, you will be able to appreciate these strengths and build on them.

CHAPTER 6 - REPROGRAMMING YOUR MIND, A NEW DIRECTION AND POSSIBLY, A NEW WAY OF LIFE

WHERE HISTORY MEETS THE PRESENT AND FUTURE

This is where history meets the present and future, prior conditioning or programming meets opportunity, where willpower meets mind power to reprogram your mind and deliver what you want in life. As alluded to in the Brain Science section, your conscious mind effectively controls your search request and the unconscious mind is the inner web of intelligence available to supply the information you need to act on, to achieve your aims and objectives. So, any changes you want to make will need to be conscious decisions that are typically programmed in four keys ways.

THE FOUR CORE METHODS FOR RE-PROGRAMMING!

We must acknowledge the fact that there are only four key ways to really make change happen:

1. Through impact – *something big that happens in your life that shocks or inspires you into making changes.*
One of mine was when we lost our second child, Lauren. She didn't survive the birth and it hit me like a rock. I dropped any and all future goals and decided to live one day at a time because that's how life comes. A surprising thing then

happened to me: I achieved levels of success and income way above what I had ever done or dreamed possible before. The weight of 'having' to have goals (I was programmed to think this way) was lifted and I just focused on being and doing the best I could every day, the achievements were not intentional but just by-products of my new higher standards of behaviour. This experience, although devastating, taught me a valuable lesson about goal setting and how it can actually be limiting in two ways, i.e. you set them too low and reach them but miss the higher opportunities that might have come if you hadn't set the goal in the first place or you set them too high and deep inside, you don't really want them badly enough or believe they're possible so your behaviour reflects this and you don't get off the starting blocks, you stall along the way or fall short and feel like a failure, even if the performance is a good one.

Goal setting is a fine balancing act and specific to each individual but for me, I don't want to limit myself by setting a certain expectation because I know if I do my best, I'll get the best results I possibly can. In this respect, I prefer to set personal 'standards' of behaviour now more than goals, although I do have a clear sense of direction for myself.

2. Through Repetition – *doing something often until it becomes a productive habit.*

I recall my early days in boxing, taking a beating nearly every week from lads that were bigger and stronger than me. I couldn't compete with their size or strengths but could make sure I got hit less and got my shots in more to pick up the points. I practised and practised and practised my footwork and my left jab in particular. These 2 aspects became my hallmarks and I went on to become county and regional area champion many times. I was even videoed so coaches could teach other kids how to 'jab & move' or if the opponent was that good 'jab & run' ☺.

I also learned early in my personal development that one reading of anything or reading without applying the knowledge was a wasted investment of both time and money because recall would be low. To recall and embed information, it requires either or both, multiple exposure and practical application so make this playbook your close companion for the next few weeks. Re-read sections, make notes or comments and apply what you learn so it becomes yours and you can then pass the baton to others so they benefit too.

3. By breaking the pattern of thought – *this is especially important if your thoughts and emotions are overwhelming you.*

My article below, published in March 2018 outlines a logical, emotionally detached method to interrupt feelings of being overwhelmed and how to alter the patterns of thoughts.
https://reecepye.com/blogs/f/logic-rules-crush-feelings-of-being-overwhelmed-in-minutes

4. Through Education – *I hated school because the subject matter was boring and if you study information that's boring to you, it will have the same effect and make no difference. So study what interests you and can help you grow stronger.*

I'm not a religious person but I am a very curious one and maybe I was looking for answers or guidance to find answers within myself after we lost Lauren so I started reading the Bible. **Ecclesiastes**, The Book of King Solomon resonated with me at the time because he said everything was like chasing after the wind and once you caught it, the power it had just dissipated. It highlighted the chase for outer pleasures versus inner peace and has stuck with me. I'm still not religious but exposing yourself to new information outside of your normal practices can open up new truths. I hope this playbook helps deliver some of these for you.

Neuroscience proves that through any or a combination of these four, the more likely it is that you will alter your brain to associate and program the new pattern of behaviour.

You can't control item 1 of course because you never know if or when such an impact might come and what kind of impact it will have on you so the most obvious route is to follow items 2 - 4, the ones you have more conscious control over. In this respect, it's a **Step Change Process,** it still gets you from the bottom of the stairs (your starting point) to the top (desired destination) but not in the one single leap that many foolish or unrealistically impatient people think is possible. Each step up acts as a firm foundation to make the next step up and the next, some may end up being bigger steps than before or you may leap two at some points but they're all in the right direction, higher and higher.

As you climb higher and higher, your view gets better and your confidence on reaching the top, stronger and stronger. The key thing is that you **resolve** to climb the first steps, have the **conviction** and **determination** to climb higher and

persist until you reach the top, the top being whatever destination you have **decided** upon.

This story of a soldier, a King and a mountain illustrates the point well.

During a battle in a war, a vigilant soldier saved a Kings life. As appreciation for this deed, the King advised the soldier to climb a mountain of his choice within the country for half a day. All the land he could view from the highest point he reached in this time would be his. The higher you climb, the more you will see and posses said the King.

The soldier hiked upwards, pausing at intervals to rest and admire the views, at each stop, the Kings officers would make notes of the most distant landmarks in all directions. The higher the soldier climbed, the more his officers could see and the larger the territory the solider could claim as his.

This sums up life in may respects because some people want the views, to claim what could be theirs but are not prepared to make the climb, even if it's just one step at a time, and then another. The higher you rise, the more opportunities you will see.

SO WHERE DO WE BEGIN WITH RE-PROGRAMMING?

In short, we start where you are now with what you know, namely: What do you want to change, remove or improve in your life. This process therefore begins with a review of your values and beliefs from your assessments. One of the problems we can often experience with the values and beliefs we hold dear is that we risk ignoring information, which is not consistent with them. In effect, we become selective (judgemental) in the way we perceive and respond to information that conflicts or contradicts with what we think.

Whilst we want to stay true to ourselves, we should consider other new, fresh and different viewpoints so as to challenge our own values and beliefs and ensure that the ones we hold, do in the fact serve us well. If we stay rigid in mindset, we can lose our 'objectivity' about the world and how we want to operate within it.

Here are six simple steps to help you challenge your thinking and if necessary some of your values and beliefs, and change any that are not serving you well:

1. Identify any behaviours that you are not happy with, ones that are not helping you get the results or outcomes you want, e.g. ask yourself the question 'What stops me being at my best or doing my best every day?'

2. Look at and list the value(s) or belief(s) that might be driving this behaviour, e.g. ask another question 'If X or Y was changed or used to drive better behaviour, what would the outcomes look like?'

3. Question it, challenge it, check where it came from, is it based on prior influences in your life, facts or just your assumptions?

4. Next decide on the actions you will take and behaviours that you wish to develop.

5. Identify and replace the ineffective thought, value, belief or behaviour with an empowering one that will support new, more effective behaviours.

6. Practice the new thinking and behaviour, repeat it and adopt it until it becomes the new habit of behaviour without conscious effort.

To help you focus on one key area of change at a time, you can also use a simple structure like this next one:

Change Action Plan (CAP).

1. The old habit I will change or eliminate:

2. The new habit I will develop or replace it with:

3. Specific first steps I will take to begin strongly:

4. To keep myself from straying or falling back into the old habit, I will enlist the help of the following practices or people:

5. My objectives and rewards linked to this new habit are:

As always, this is just one effective way to help embed changes and whilst it's a good guideline, you can adapt it for your style of doing things to ensure you get the best results. The FROM – TO chapter later in this playbook will also help you change old and create new habits.

WHAT DO NEAR DEATH EXPERIENCES (NDE), USING THE PARALLEL UNIVERSE METHOD OF REFLECTION OR THE TRUMAN SHOW HAVE IN COMMON?

When your values, beliefs and subsequent thinking patterns have been part of you for so long, it can be difficult to step outside of yourself and look in objectively but the following technique can help you do this.

To see for yourself that you are not your thoughts or your emotions, that they are in fact just part of the whole you, try the following exercise based on stories of people who had near death experiences (NDE). These are people who've had 'out of body' experiences and then later relayed back what happened, sometimes in chillingly accurate detail, what doctors and nurses did to revive them from death and bring them back to life, they could also recall who in their family was there and what they said and did too.

The following article sheds new light (no pun intended) on what happens after death and kind of makes me think it's not dissimilar to when you click the off switch where your cable is plugged into the wall but the green light where the cable connects to your MacBook stays lit for a while, albeit temporarily until the charge runs out.

https://bigthink.com/philip-perry/after-death-youre-aware-that-youve-died-scientists-claim

It could also be the imagination at play and whilst I have no opinion as to whether the stories are true or false, it did get me thinking about how we can consciously use our imagination to illustrate the separation from our thoughts.

TRY THIS SIMPLE EXERCISE

Close your eyes and imagine yourself stepping outside of your body and moving to the corner of a room or a position where you can see the physical you.

When there, look in on yourself.
What kind of person do you see?
What thoughts do you see arising from your mind?
If you were to give yourself some advice about anything, what would it be?

You can play with different scenarios, such as imagining yourself in a business meeting, past present or future because imagination is a powerful tool for reflection, grounding yourself in the present and projecting forward to potential behaviours in the future, e.g.

Past – Reviewing how you acted, contributed or otherwise and what you would have done differently.

Present – As a way to jolt yourself out of a non-productive state of mind and into a positive one whilst at the meeting so you make the kind of impact you want and not later on after the meeting has finished, regretting that you didn't act in the way you felt you could or should have at the time.

Future – Play it forward, although you can't predict the future and how others may act in meetings or events, you can set yourself up for the way in which you will behave. This is especially the case if you know there are going to be difficult or confrontational people attending who would previously have got your emotions heated.

An alternative way to do this is to imagine you're in a **Parallel Universe;** everything is the same except you're now looking in from the outside. As with the **NDE** method, you can apply the same questions and observations from the above exercise. If you were in the parallel universe, how would you change what you see in this one?

The Truman Technique is another way you can look at your life as it is, which I named after The Truman Show starring Jim Carrey. Are you living a life of reality or illusion and if you were watching your own show (life) how would you feel or change it. This article about the Truman Show 20 Year Anniversary Interviews in Vanity Fair is both telling and worrying. It demonstrates how imagination can often become reality so be careful what you wish for.

https://www.vanityfair.com/hollywood/2018/06/truman-show-anniversary-jim-carrey-peter-weir-laura-linney

"Imagination is more important than knowledge, for knowledge is limited to all we know and understand, while imagination embraces the whole world, and all there ever will be to know and understand" Albert Einstein

In effect, if 'you' become aware of your thoughts and emotions, then 'you' must be separate from them. At first this may seem hard to grasp but how often have you caught your thoughts and stopped them, in effect you become conscious of what you were previously unconsciously thinking or feeling?

If you can observe or imagine your thoughts, then the thoughts are not you but only part of you and if they are only part of you, then these parts can be managed and controlled, BY YOU!

It's about **waking up** to reality, what's here now and being **alert** to and **aware** of your thoughts and feelings so that you monitor, manage and control them and not the other way around. This means being conscious of what you're thinking and doing more and more often.

For now, make it your aim to notice what's going on in and around you more often. It may be difficult at first and you may only 'wake up' to this once or twice a day but the more often you do this, the easier it will become and the more you will notice how much you are in control of your mind and that it no longer has the hold on you that it did before.

In effect, becoming more conscious more often enables you to circumvent 'auto-pilot' syndrome where your mind wanders and thinks all on its own to control you - instead, you can turn the tables and consciously take control of 'it'.

YOU get to hack your mind by knowing what tricks it tries to play on you and how it will resist the changes so it can try to stay in command – you effectively become the command centre for the mind and not the other way around any longer.

By doing this, any and all non-beneficial or damaging thought situations like the following, can become things of the past, they stay in the past and no longer trouble you in the present:

Confusion or indecision

Excessive thinking

Emotional Hijacks

Feeling of Overwhelm

Anger or aggression

Resentments or regrets

Fear, doubt, worry, anxiety

Comparisons, envy, jealousy

Judging

Sometimes, thoughts like these can be like a raging river and you're caught up in it but when you become consciously aware, it's like standing on the riverbank watching the torrents (thoughts) passing by from a distance, a more objective and controlled place…. And you stay dry!

For many and maybe you're one of the many, dissolving damaging feelings caused by the above is a breakthrough because it clears the path for all the good stuff to come, and which you can build on for greater benefit.

To become conscious means exactly that, becoming conscious!

Initially, you may only become truly conscious of your thoughts and emotions a few times a day but with self-discipline and practice this will improve and get easier and easier day-by-day. By doing this consistently every day, you will build a muscle in your mind that dances to the drum of your conscious decisions and not your unconscious programming. You can be sure that the previous programming will put up quite a fight to stay in control because you're invading it's territory so to speak but you don't have to fight it, simple work around it by creating new, more effective neural connections in your brain. You will notice day by day that you have a clearer picture of who you really are and a clearer vision of who you will become, based on your true inner values and not what society sets up as the statue to worship.

It take practice, practice and then more practice and few master the ability to stay conscious and take control of this thing called our brain but those who want change badly enough are those who stick with it, benefiting greatly with peace of mind and a sincere gratitude for the ability to control their thoughts and emotions through the miracle power of their mind.

When we 'switch on' our conscious mind, it's far easier and more effective to retain what's useful, discard what's useless and then add our own originality (authenticity) to what is especially beneficial to our being, in effect, it's a simple process of debugging, re-programming and setting the software (our thinking and emotional controls) to be the most advantageous as possible.

"Keep your conscious mind focused on what you want and your unconscious mind will unerringly guide you to it" *Napoleon Hill*

This is where mindfulness and meditation are coming to the fore more often in society today because these practices help focus attention on the present reality and essentially, this is what being conscious is about.

MINDFULNESS & MEDITATION

Much has been shared about these two aspects of mind management and yet there is still much in the way of misguided assumptions. Many believe that they are two of the same thing and that the core principle is to 'quieten' the mind, to empty it of all thoughts to reach a state of inner calmness but this is only partly true compared with the bigger picture. In reality, **mindfulness** is exactly what is says, being mindful (consciously noticing) what's going on in and around you but without any form of emotional reaction, attachment or judgement. It means observing and concentrating on the present, which can mean decisions in the present that have an impact on the future, e.g. being mindful of what impact decisions made now may have on you and others later. The best explanation of mindfulness I ever heard was **"Wherever you are, be there"** which means being fully in the moment and not just being there physically whilst being somewhere else mentally.

Meditation on the other hand is more about mental relaxation that helps decrease metabolism, lowers blood pressure, and improves heart rate and brain waves through breathing exercises. In effect, it helps tension and tightness to seep from muscles as the body receives a **quiet** message to relax from the brain.

Many studies show that the practice of **meditation**, carried out on a regular basis, can significantly reduce or mitigate the symptoms of stress and anxiety. It helps stop excessive thinking to put the mind back in order, often allowing people to start thinking again from a fresh start.

If you've never tried meditation or have tried it unsuccessfully before, try again with a different mindset, e.g. short guided meditations are a good place to start and the following can help:

Finding Peace in a Frantic World by Mark Williams & Danny Penman, which has a selection of meditations ranging from just 3 minutes up to 15 minutes. You can find them on YouTube or via the link below.

http://franticworld.com/free-meditations-from-mindfulness/

Alternatively or additionally, for a wider range of meditations, Headspace is a very popular app to download from.

THE SURPRISE MEDITATION FROM A BUDDHIST SESSION

I did some field research on Buddhism recently and attended a session as part of a course called **'How to solve our human problems'**, led by a Senior Buddhist Nun from the Kadampa Buddhist Foundation.

This may sound a bit deep but actually it wasn't at all, it was quite a surprise to be honest. Far from my (inaccurate) assumption that they would meditate to clear and quieten the mind, they actually focused on recognising and accepting a particular problem (note they call it what it is, a problem and not a challenge) in mind-set and dealing with it.

The problem chosen to focus on was anger and how to deal with it mentally in terms of a person holding anger in their own mind or anger coming from another person. Part of the process was meditation, part instruction, and part discussion about how to dissolve and eliminate the power this emotion had on you. I was curious to learn their ways and came away with a new viewpoint on Buddhism (no, I'm not converted, just better informed now) because the method was not the kind of 'spiritual' meditation many might think of, e.g. sitting with legs crossed, pinching your fingers and humming to yourself but dealing with real life issues relevant to todays chaotic world.

In effect, the Kadampa Buddhist approach is to become conscious of the unconscious, to wake up, become alert to and aware of our thoughts and feelings more often instead of running on autopilot. It completely turns the table on some people's views about trying to ignore the problems and just using will power to try and move on. This often means that the problem thought and feeling continues to linger whilst you're trying to move forward and consequently, you keep being pulled back or down.

But you can't solve a problem you don't see so becoming aware is the first step, i.e. bringing conscious awareness to a particular problem thought or feeling and being able to take a logical and emotionally detached approach to dealing with it.

Another Buddhist Surprise
The video below demonstrates that every human being has challenges, even Buddhist Monks.
https://www.youtube.com/watch?v=lR9sLgefBAU
These Monk stories illustrate that no-one is perfect and no-one said it better than Professor Stephen Hawking.

"One of the basic rules of the universe is that NOTHING IS PERFECT. Perfection simply doesn't exist… without imperfection, neither you or I would exist"

So, if things don't go to plan straight away or you see yourself (self-observation) falling back into former habits, don't beat yourself up. Stay on the road, you're bound to come across some internal fights but persist because it is sincere **Q**uestioning, **A**ssessment, **K**nowledge and **A**ction **(Q.A.K.A)** on what you're learning that will overcome resistance.

THE TRUTH ABOUT YOU

I am not perfect, you are not perfect but this does not stop us from improving who and where we are, we can build on our **Strengths** and reduce or eliminate the impact of our **Weaknesses.**

This is an area I've focused on and taught colleagues and direct reports to apply so that they don't waste valuable time strengthening weaknesses but use their energy to make more us of their strengths.

The above phrase 'The Truth About You' was the title of a book written by one of the founders of the Strengths Movement, called Marcus Buckingham. He was a senior researcher and executive at the Gallup Organisation that developed the **Strengths Finder** assessment tool. He then founded his own company and created a new strengths finding assessment tool called **Standout,** which in my experience has been the most accurate tool I've ever used. In his book, Marcus pointed out that a true strength is not just something you're good at but something that you also love doing, it energises you and makes you feel stronger as person. A weakness on the other hand is any activity that leaves you feeling weaker, you loath doing it. These are the things you need to remove from your life or at least reduce if you are to maximise results using your strengths.

Marcus suggested keeping a small pad (and provided one with his book) to record activities and times during the day when you felt 'strengthened' by what you did or 'weakened' by it so that you could see where your energy was best invested and what to try and build on or eliminate in future. You may want to try it yourself and have the following on the front and back of each sheet on the pad.

I loved it (felt strong, energised, excited) when... then write the specific activity you loved. Record only one activity per page.

I loathed it (felt weak, drained, bored) when... then write the specific activity you loathed. Record only one activity per page.

At the end of the day and week or month, separate and group the pages and you'll have a good picture of where you're investing your time that serves you or shrinks you. A strength I was renowned for as a Head of Sales was in the analysis of reporting spreadsheets and noticing errors or trends almost immediately but it drained me, I absolutely hated doing it. Prior to reading 'The truth About You' and shifting my view (my thinking) of what a strength really was, I just considered the above task as part of my role and did it.

After doing the above exercise however, I developed my exec assistant to take more responsibility for this task and she not only did a fantastic job but also willingly took on the task to help herself grow in this area! It didn't remove the need for me to review the spreadsheets completely but it reduced the work and time I spent on them dramatically.

Use the ideas and techniques I've offered but also use whatever tech may be right for you, alarms, reminder, calendar scheduling, make appointments with and for yourself to focus on strengths and eliminate the *impact* of weaknesses. By doing this, you will achieve successes in your desired areas and not always what others seek of or expect of you, you'll be doing what you love for yourself.

"Everybody is a genius. But if you judge a fish by it's ability to climb a tree, it will live its whole life believing that it is stupid" *Albert Einstein*

Up Next

How to overcome obstacles or barriers to success and deal with the biggest obstacle of all.

CHAPTER 7 - OVERCOMING OBSTACLES & BARRIERS TO SUCCESS

THE SINGLE BIGGEST OBSTACLE WE HAVE TO DEAL WITH IS FORMED FROM OUR PAST PROGRAMMING AND IS OF COURSE, OUR 'HABITUAL' THOUGHTS AND BEHAVIOURS!

If you're not aware of these resistances in advance of trying out new ideas and ways of thinking, they can have a **HABIT** of stopping you in your tracks or creeping back in to disrupt progress when you least expect it.

Because of the way you're going to question existing programmed thinking, it's easy to discard new ideas without giving conscious consideration to trying them out. There can be a natural resistance to new ideas and truths that go something like this:

1st Exposure – Rejection because it conflicts with our current (programmed) thinking

2nd Exposure – Resistance because whilst it makes sense, we can't (emotionally) accept it

3rd Exposure – Partial Acceptance because whilst we understand it, we have reservations about applying it, we question if it will work for us

Changing Mindsets – Changing Results

4th Exposure – Acceptance because we're willing to try it out and our current way is not working well enough, it kind of resonates with us and we can foresee some benefits

5th Exposure – Full Understanding because we've used it and it works

6th Exposure – Ownership, the idea belongs to us now and we feel comfortable sharing it with others because we have proven it for ourselves.

As mentioned earlier, reprogramming can be driven in a number of ways but often, the most effective way to make improvements (I prefer the word improvement to change) is through repetition that creates a new habit or replaces an old ineffective habit with a new and more empowering one. In this respect, the understanding of how our brain works and the use of mind hacks as a concept for positive change is just a starting point, as it helps us to realise, we have more potential control than we're currently utilising.

The difficult task is building on the programming from the past that is good, recognising parts of programming that could be improved and of course, identifying those parts of our currently programmed mind that do us harm and need to be removed, dissolved or changed completely.

SYSTEM BUGS & DEBUGGING

As we've covered already, just like a computer system, our brain or inner computer runs on software (our values, beliefs, principles which drive our thoughts, feelings and behaviours) and with any system or software, there are bugs. These are the negatives that have (previously) gotten in our way but which, through conscious control and the use of creative logical imagination, we can fix, disable or remove from our personalities for good.

However, you can't solve a problem you don't know you have so you must become aware of the kind of bugs (habits) that reside in your mind, the things that literally bug you and get in the way of your progress. Also be aware that these bugs can creep back in unconsciously so be alert to this possibility so you can deal with them. You will therefore need to remain vigilant in your quest for positive change. Typical 'bugs' come in the form of thoughts that generate an emotional reaction, e.g. How often have you felt emotions like these, feel free to add your own:

Fear,

Anger,

Aggression,

Anxiety,

Doubt,

Indecision,

Depression

FEAR is obviously a biggie when it comes to re-programming because as humans, we're cautious to avoid anything that might hurt us, whether it be physically or psychologically. This is where the protective Amygdala comes into play.

Typically, the main form of fear is psychological and not physical, such as fear of:

Failure,

Making mistakes,

Embarrassing ourselves,

Being inadequate,

Being seen as a fake,

Change,

Uncertainty,

Rejection,

Missing Out,

Losing Control,

Feeling Stupid,

Add your own…

We will all experience some or all of these at some stage in our lives, I certainly have but I'm still alive and kicking. If they're not controlled however, they can make cowards of us unnecessarily, especially if we've been raised in an environment that focuses heavily on perfection, which was much of my early conditioning. This makes us hesitant and discourages us from taking the actions we wanted for fear and risk of making mistakes. We fear making mistakes so we don't do anything! Taking action can sometimes mean entering into the unknown and whilst we may be uncomfortable with it, taking no action just leaves us a) where we are already and b) probably feeling even worse about ourselves because the knock-on effect is that one fear triggers many of the others from the above list. This re-enforces the neural connections in a negative way, making it harder still to change them later on. So, the sooner you apply the process of re-programming and the formulas I've shared with you, the easier it will become to make improvements you want and the faster these changes will become your new habits.

NB. Here's the thing about psychological fear, it's exactly that, psychological and not real, it's made up in our own minds and we now know that we have the capability to 'change our minds' literally.

FEAR is therefore overrated and over-estimated because most often times, the fear doesn't transpire. For many people, it's disabling them even though it's not real, it's a series of emotions (neural connections via the synapses) programmed into the unconscious and which, can be re-programmed with new connections through the conscious mind.

Lack of self-confidence, low self-esteem and poor self-belief are all by-products of fear, and there's another consideration to the obstacle that negative thoughts or emotions present as well.

ANGER as a bug and which comes in many forms, such as aggression, resentment, annoyance, frustration, rage, displeasure, hostility, dissatisfaction, bitterness, hatred and more.

For those of you who drive (and passengers have often seen this) have you ever gotten angry that someone wouldn't make way for you, jumped across or cut in front of you and you instantly reacted with anger and aggression, maybe recently even?

You raised your fist, stuck one or two fingers up, maybe even tried to cut them up as a lesson, possibly even putting your family in danger (you'd lost any thought for them in this moment of rage) because mentally you were in another place – revenge! And then you see in the other car, that it's an old lady who looks extremely worried and a bit lost – guilt, shame, self-defeating emotions flood your mind and you feel like a bully.

Or

You see in the other car, that it's a big burly bloke with a face that looks like thunder – fear, regret, apprehension of what might happen and again, self-defeating emotions flood your mind and you feel like a coward.

Life is full of many other situations like this but the over-riding thing when reacting unconsciously rather than responding consciously is that it damages our inner being. We've acted in a way that is not in-sync with who we truly believe we are or want to be and by this I mean, how we know is the right and proper, constructive and productive way for us to behave.

It's a highly destructive feeling that can eat away at us and make us feel like we're less than we truly are inside, it's crippling to our self-esteem and our growth. The same thing hits us hard when we say one thing to somebody but mean another, it hurts us deep inside doesn't it and unwittingly, we re-enforce these feelings through self-talk that takes over our mind. 'Why didn't I say something, why am I so dumb or cowardly, what stopped me being truthful, now the situation is worse than before'... it can spiral out of control and one single negative thought ends up triggering a whole new set of connections in the brain, ouch!

How and where have these been of help to you in your life, in your relationship with yourself or with others and especially loved ones we hold near and dear.

So often, we hold these incongruent thoughts and emotions in our heads and the other person or people they're focused on have no idea, they're oblivious and carrying on their lives whilst we continue with harmful emotions.

Take a look at the following story of **'Two Monks, a Woman and a River'** because it illustrates how we carry negative thoughts and emotions unnecessarily.
https://www.youtube.com/watch?v=8JVIVbLXqFo

It's not surprising therefore:
- That despite the fact we live in a world with more potential for personal growth and wealth creation than probably at any other time in history, so many people achieve so little and lead lives far below what they truly know they're capable of.
- That we have so few people willing to buck the trend and have the self-confidence or conviction to be different and dance to the beat of a different drum.
- That the majority continue to conform and compare their life with the norm, there's nothing wrong with that but normal is average and you don't have to be average if you don't want to be.
- That people with a desire to be themselves, buckle to the society version rather than stand up or speak up for what's right for themselves.
- That so many people begin the journey but don't persist past the first difficulty and quickly go back to their old shape. They're like elastic bands that get pulled out of shape and expanded by new information only to go back to their comfort zones and fall back into old conditioned shape.

No human being with any common sense would deliberately harm themselves in this way would they, so... we must acknowledge that they (we) are doing so unconsciously, through our pre-conditioned and pre-programmed self. The good news for you is that you now know that you can re-program your brain and its software consciously.

There are too many obstacles to cover in this short playbook but you have the foundation to make the changes you want by being aware of some of the main ones, you can now begin to turn this knowledge into personal power. Ultimately, it's about you making a conscious decision to cut off from the past and move forward in the ways that are true for you. Although very simple in structure, I've found the following formula to be dramatically effective in identifying, dissolving and overcoming obstacles.

https://reecepye.com/blogs/f/smarter-problem-analysing-decision-making-%E2%80%93-using-socd

INNER PEACE OF MIND & OUTER SUCCESS IS AN ELIMINATION PROCESS

One of the biggest mistakes I see in business and in life in general, is that some (most even) people try to add 'things' to become mentally stronger or more successful in life and ignore the things that hold them back. Not dealing with such obstacles can leave you confused about why you're not making the progress you want. Ray Dalio, an American billionaire investor and philanthropist is one of the most successful hedge fund mangers in history and his simple 5-step formula for new graduates (or anyone for that matter) to succeed in life includes two of the key principles he's followed to become so successful https://www.principles.com/

'Spot the roadblocks that will stop you from getting where you want to be and look deeper into the problem'

What's next?

In the following section you will find an effective method for moving from a negative emotional state of mind to a positive one. It's an adaption from one of the most successful books ever written on the subject of self-image psychology and which has sold over 30 million copies worldwide.

CHAPTER 8 - MOVING YOU 'FROM-TO'

IN THIS CHAPTER, YOU'LL LEARN HOW TO TURN A NEGATIVE FRAME OF MIND INTO A POSITIVE ONE, INSTANTLY.

If you were to ask anyone I've worked with if I was lacking in confidence or lazy, you'd get a resounding no or a rhetorical question that goes something like 'Are you kidding me?' and yet their view of me wouldn't be entirely accurate. They may well have that perception of me but the reality is very different, I did suffer from self-doubt and I was lazy. Whilst these may be perceived to be negatives, they were actually turned into very constructive and productive positives. Let me explain:

SELF-DOUBT

Based on my upbringing, it was hardly surprising that I was an insecure little kid and the early programming stayed with me into my work. But, because I doubted myself, it made me want to be more knowledgeable and better prepared than anyone that I wanted or needed to influence in my career. So, I studied all kinds of business books, invested in learning about management psychology, key account sales, business process, change management and always tried to be one step ahead, using the following **'3 Step CRT Influence Process'** that enabled me to ethically influence others, namely:

Credibility – Show rather than just tell people that you're credible in the chosen area for discussion.

Respect – Earn their respect by creatively challenging 'conventional or outdated' thinking, help add to their knowledge and provide good advice and support.

Trust – This can only be accomplished if you make the other two happen first, in that order because you can't earn respect if you're not credible in your field. It requires that after showing them you're 'ahead of the pack' you stay there by continuing to study, learn and add value to the relationship.

LAZINESS – I just hate to waste valuable energy, either physically or mentally, it just eats away at me if things don't get done properly or efficiently, with speed.

I like to get things out of the way so I can move onto the next thing, the next task, satisfy the next desire or value and this may give the impression (wrongly so) that I'm fast and furious in my actions, I rush to get things sorted. This assumption is wholly inaccurate however because I employ a **'slow down to speed up'** ethic here. Rather than rush in, I step back, take a close look at what needs to be achieved, what could possibly derail me on the way, who I need to get behind my plans, how to deal with potential obstacles and then implement with speed and follow through to successful completion with minimum fuss. It means I rarely need to go back and re-do work again, it saves me masses of time and satisfies my lazy (positive lazy) character trait. In this respect, the following FROM – TO formula I came across can help you to turn negatives into positives too.

HOW TO CHANGE A NEGATIVE FRAME OF MIND TO A POSITIVE ONE, INSTANTLY! YOUR EMOTIONS NEEDN'T STAY FIXED AND HERE'S WHY.

Whatever stage in life you're at, it's easy to get hijacked by doubtful emotions or tough situations and get into a mental fight to try and overcome them. You second-guess your thinking, your direction, your decisions, your actions and emotions can get in your way but you don't have to fight them… just learn to go with them to another place, a better place, instantly!

I first came across an idea called FROM-TO many years ago when I was a young adult myself studying psychology. I purchased an audio program based on a best selling book called **Psycho-Cybernetics,** which has now sold in excess of 30 million copies globally.

It was written by a famous plastic surgeon that made the physical adjustments people wanted, only to find that despite the cosmetic changes, his clients still had the same psychological problems after surgery.

This raised the question of how to move people from the negatively conditioned feelings they had about themselves and their situations to the positive ones they desired, hence the FROM-TO methodology.

As a society, we've set up a world of contrast, good or bad, high or low, wealthy or poor, right or wrong, success or failure… in essence a life of either this or that, so it's not surprising then, that our brains are programmed to think this way.

However, we can use these exact same contrasts to move us from where we are now to where we want to be, by applying logic and emotions together for combined power.

Most people consider emotions as part of who they are rather than as feelings that we can control, providing of course that we understand 'how' to divert unwanted emotions and feelings. By doing so, we can begin to harness their power and control them rather than them controlling us!

"To change a habit, make a conscious decision, then act out the new behaviour" *Maxwell Maltz — Psycho-Cybernetics*

We come to understand that emotions are not real except in our own minds and if we decide to change our minds, we can change our emotions, we just need a process for doing this effectively.

For most of my working life, I've viewed emotions as energy in motion (E-Motion) namely, that which moves us and the way we feel. I've used this understanding to sell millions of pounds worth of advertising to brand name buyers and their agencies every year and lead teams that have sold tens of millions to the same kind of buyers every year. Believe me when I say that these are tough people to influence. An emotion is therefore mental energy that not only influences our own behaviour but also influences those we communicate with daily, emotions that drive us and others, lifting us up or pulling us down, propelling us forward or pushing us back, getting a yes or getting a no.

A major resistance to changing our emotions and improving our states of mind so they serve us rather than us serving them is that we try to use will power alone to overcome the negative emotional habits. We try to do this in our heads and this often creates frustrations because of conflicting thoughts and values whirling around and the usual fight between the conscious and unconscious mind.

I found early on in my career that the best way to change them is not to resist them or fight them in our minds but to take them out of our heads and apply the contrasting emotions in a conscious logical way. In this respect, you could say that **LOGIC RULES** because you're taking a conscious and rational approach to an emotional issue.

THIS IS WHERE THE 'FROM-TO' FORMULA CAN WORK FOR YOUR BENEFIT.

It's a quick and simple way to divert your focus away from one emotion you don't like or which doesn't serve you well to one that does, i.e. simplicity itself because it's a practical exercise that only takes minutes or even seconds to use depending on the nature of the 'problem' mental state and your own unique circumstances of course.

You don't have to dream big or try to change the world, just decide to change 'your' world as it is right now, one emotion at a time and improve your situation, then improve some more and then some more and before you know it, you'll be flying high and fast. Just take a sheet of paper and draw a line down the middle or create a word doc or PowerPoint if you wish (example below and more examples provided at the end of this chapter).

FROM 'OLD' – TO 'NEW'

FROM 'OLD'	TO 'NEW'
Hesitancy & Doubt	Conviction & Belief
Inertia	Action
Fear	Courage & Confidence
Easily Distracted	Focused & Disciplined
Restless & On Edge	Calm & Relaxed
Lethargic	Motivated & Active
Unfulfilled	Fulfilled
Discontent	Happy
Tomorrow	Today
Going Nowhere / Being No-One	Going Places / Being Special

Produced by: Reece Pye – www.reecepye.com

⇒ On the left hand side write FROM at the top and on the right hand side, write TO at the top.

⇒ Then write the negative emotions in the left column and counter these with the opposite, productive emotions in the right column.

⇒ Whenever you feel one or a combination of the emotions in the left hand column, refer to the FROM-TO sheet, read, recognise and accept the emotion on the left but then read the counter-emotion in the right hand column so you focus on the desired emotional habit you want to create.

⇒ Add power to this by closing your eyes for a few seconds to picture in your mind through conscious imagination, a situation where you're applying and behaving in the desired way based on the right hand emotion.

"Imagination is everything, it is the preview of life's coming attractions" *Albert Einstein*

I have my own slant on what imagination really is and how it can work well with the FROM-TO method, namely: Imagination is really made up of two words: Imagine and Action and that's the way we should view it so the images in our mind results in action, and the action produces the desired result.

"The true sign of intelligence is not knowledge but imagination" *Albert Einstein*

If we only create an image in our mind and it stays there, nothing happens does it, we need to take that image and do something with it, turn it into something that produces the results we want.

"Logic will get you from A to B. Imagination will take you everywhere" *Albert Einstein*

We all have our own ways of working so test different times and places to refer to the sheet, e.g. first thing in the morning to start the day off well, midday by way of reminder, early evening or last thing at night before you go to sleep to tap into your unconscious.

Why do I quote Albert Einstein so often in relation to the use of imagination?

Because he was a Physician believed to have an IQ of 160 and you'd typically think (old programmed brain thinking) that everything he did would revolve around logic, rational thought, facts, structure rather than free thought but it wasn't. He tapped into a higher intelligence, one we all possess but rarely use, other than for fearful imaginations in the case of some people. Another great man with an IQ of 160 (the late Professor Stephen Hawking) also knew the power of his mind and imagination, and if you haven't already watched the film **'The Theory of Everything'** starring Eddie Redmayne and Benedict Cumberbatch, I'd recommend it.

"Although I cannot move and I have to speak through a computer, in my mind I am free." Professor Stephen Hawking

The wonderful thing about imagination is that you don't have to do any hard thinking; you just picture in your mind the desired outcomes. These images penetrate the conscious to go straight into the unconscious and the more you practice, the more it registers and becomes a part of you.

You'll be surprised that by what you picture on the inside, you begin to notice more on the outside because of your focus, e.g. opportunities, situations, things that align to what you want to be or to happen, it's your **RAS** at work for your benefit and not to your detriment. Imagination is obviously a creative thing (to create) so use whatever method works best for you. Whatever you choose though, persist because persistence will beat resistance!!!

"**We are what we repeatedly do. Excellence (success) then is not an act, but a habit we must acquire".** Aristotle

Therefore, don't expect to change your ways in one reading or two or three, or even one, two or three attempts. It takes a little time and conscious effort to make the changes but when you do, they become part of a better you.

Just bear in mind the single most effective method of control you have to change or create a new habit is using repetition and persistence until the changes become automatic, habitual, part of the new you.

Start eliminating the OLD and replacing with the NEW today!

The power of changing just one emotion or one set of linked emotions can change your situation (maybe even your life or part of it, like work maybe) for the better and help you make the progress you want.

'**FROM-TO' TEMPLATES** You can see a few more detailed 'FROM-TO' editable templates in the following pages.

FROM - TO

Procrastinating – Avoiding the things that I know must be done if I'm to move forward but are also difficult, uncomfortable, I don't like doing!	Proactive – Get real, holding back doesn't help me, anticipate the desired results and take one action today to get going!
Confusion & Indecision – I don't have all the facts, I need to research some more, I'm still getting ready,! I have this sense of uncertainty about the future.	Clear Focus & Decisive – I don't need more facts or research. What I know is good, I'm ready to begin with what I have, now.
Fearful – Of failure or what people may think, say or do.	Bravery & Courage – To trust in myself, it's my life and the people who love and respect me will still love and respect me, regardless.
Frustrated – At not using the God given talent I posses, wasting my time and my life	Satisfaction & Fulfillment – This is the big one for me because I know I'm talented, I have done good stuff before and I'm going to again, starting today!

Produced by: Reece Pye – www.reecepye.com

FROM - TO

Continually living or dragging up the past, including resentments	Accepting what's gone before and looking ahead to a better place
Sitting here alone, doing nothing but thinking, hesitating, doubting myself	Deciding to at least try, one thing at a time, getting stronger with each action
Allowing my mind and emotions to dictate how I feel, controlling me	Being conscious of my ability to choose what I focus on
Looking for the quick and easy way, the routes of least resistance, short-term thinking	Doing what's tougher now but I know will make life easier and more rewarding in the longer term
Avoiding tough decisions and changing nothing about my situation	Considering my choices, the consequences of each one and acting on the best one available to me right now
Continually aiming for perfection that inevitably stops me from fulfilling my capabilities	Do what is good enough to achieve my objective and continue to improve along the way
Concentrating my energies on barriers and reasons not to act or move ahead	Concentrating energies on opportunities and compelling reasons to do something

Produced by: Reece Pye – www.reecepye.com

Changing Mindsets – Changing Results   *www.ReecePye.com*

FROM "I do not" – TO "Instead I"

Cringe or winge	Create what I want in life
Bottle it	Draw on my inner strengths, convictions
Take unnecessary s**t from people	Stand up, give as good as I get
Cave in / Give up easily	Fight for my cause, my family, my sanity
Worry about what others 'may' think of me	Concentrate my attention on what I think of myself
Hesitate through being unsure or insecure	I follow my own path and own it fully
Continually aim for perfection that inevitably stops me from fulfilling my capabilities	Do what is good enough to achieve my objective and continue to improve along the way
Allow myself to be the captive of my thinking habits and conditioned to stay as I am	Act as the person I've always wanted to be and undo the conditioning of the past

Produced by: Reece Pye – www.reecepye.com

FROM "I do not" – TO "Instead I"

Assume, Judge or Criticise others	Investigate, discover and understand
Use the force of persuasion or try to convince people in ways that are good for me but not for them	Influence by asking, understanding and helping others with absolute integrity so that the benefits are mutual
Doubt I have knowledge and value to share	Use my voice to actively share with others
Give up my time and energy freely	Choose who is deserving of my help
Waste my time trying to sell to people	I educate people so they can make their own decisions to buy from me
Fear technology or social media communications	I embrace what's new, learn from it and use it for everyone's advantage
Have to control everything and everyone in my life	Control only what is necessary and go with the flow with other things, I relax more
Ignore the obvious trends nor become victim to the herd mentality	Use trends to my advantage and avoid herd mentality by following my own inner values

Produced by: Reece Pye – www.reecepye.com

Changing Mindsets – Changing Results   *www.ReecePye.com*

SO WHAT HAPPENS NOW?

SUMMARY & SUCCESS ESSENTIALS

We've covered a lot of ground within this program and there could be many areas you'd like to work on to improve.

The danger here is that you pick too many to work on at once and end up diluting the impact or it becomes just too much to chew in one go and you end up choking and not doing any areas very well.

My recommendation is to pick one or two key areas you'd like to work on initially and concentrate on these until you see the measurable progress you want or the change is embedded and working effectively on positive autopilot.

At this point, you're probably thinking to yourself 'how long do I have to focus on something until I see the change I want?' and that's natural because 'mentally' it will give us satisfaction in knowing.

But this is the old programmed part of the brain kicking in again. The reality is that it takes different amounts of time for different people and their different challenges. Maxwell Maltz in his book **Psycho-Cybernetics** stated that 'typically' it took 21 days to form a new habit but that's a generic answer based on the law of averages from his patients in a different era of time.

Attention spans are lower now than ever before but we tend to take in more information more easily than ever before as well, so for some, working on something every day for 21 consecutive days could be a bit tiresome, we need variety and want speedy results. With this in mind you may want to 'chunk' improvements and alternate multiple items, e.g. let's say you pick 4 key areas to work on. You could chunk these into a week at a time so that you work on all 4 within a month. If you then repeat the process, you will have worked on the four key areas three times within just one quarter and probably given more concentration to each one for 3 full weeks, timed by 7 days per week equals the 21 days.

It all depends on the nature of the 'thing' you want to change or improve, how deeply embedded (programmed) it is as part of you, your level of desire, determination and discipline to follow through on the change and so on.

With the technology available to us today, e.g. smartphones with alarms, alerts, calendars and scheduling capability, we have the tools to learn these new habits faster than ever before. You could even put it as the lock-screen message on your phone. According to recent research, we unlock our screen an average of 110 times each day so this would give maximum exposure to the new habit you want to embed and with minimum effort. Whichever the case, the following framework should help to set you on your way and act as an ongoing summary reference tool to stay on track.

THE 'SIX-FIGURE SUCCESS ESSENTIALS' FRAMEWORK

So called because it's the framework I used to earn six-figure incomes early in my business career and subsequently to coach teams and business owners to increase monthly revenues by six-figures, and in some cases to make seven figure annual revenue impacts.

It's worked for me and my hope is that it will act as a good guide for you too, one that has proven universally successful but also allows the flexibility to add any elements of your choosing and that suit your own style of doing things.

1. Your Values

Be clear about your values in each area of your life and prioritise them. Your highest values become your most prized motivators and instil a strong internal drive, which in turn, leads to action and direction, just like a compass.

2. Clear Aspirations & Objectives

Decide what is it that you want to accomplish, whether it be tangible, intangible or a combination of both. Once you've decided, commit to it and take the very first action as soon as possible to begin building momentum.

3. Your Belief System

If you don't believe you are capable or worthy of accomplishing what you've set out to do, you will either not start or limit your success. Identify any limiting beliefs and consciously shift them by seeing the positive outcomes and rewards instead. Set the belief system that serves yours needs.

4. Plan (As Far As You Can See)

You can't always see all the required steps at the start of a journey but you can plan as far as you can see right now. Set out your plan and start moving. As you accomplish more and more, you'll come to bends in the road and be able to see around them and what needs to be done further ahead.

5. Continue to Educate Yourself

Adding to your knowledge that others don't have will set you apart, increasing your competence, confidence and levels of success. As mentioned earlier in the playbook, don't rely solely on your company training because this will be same as everyone else gets and is therefore unlikely to make you any different to anyone else.

Instead, look in new places and explore quick and easy ways to learn, like Soundview Executive Book Summaries www.summary.com, compressed non-fiction books via www.getabstract.com or Harvard Business Reviews www.HBR.ORG articles as these take complete books and condense them into just a few pages.

For learning on the go, consider audio books as an addition or alternative and www.audible.com is a good provider or www.scribd.com which offers books, magazines and audio at one of the lowest monthly subscription prices on the market today.

Continuous Learning = Continuous Personal Growth and Success,
Education increases competence,
Competence increases confidence,
Confidence increases belief,
Belief increases desire,
Desire increases motivation… and so on.

Which all effectively create new productive neural connections that deliver an awesome collective impact.

6. Remain Flexible

Keep your eyes focused on what you want to accomplish but be flexible in your approach and adapt if you need to along the way. Your strength will come from your ability to bend with strong winds and not be rigid enough for the wind to break you or knock you down.

7. Persist

Do not allow any obstacles to steal your thunder, resolve to persist to the end and accomplish what you've set out to, unless better opportunities come up that suit your needs even more of course. Whatever the case, persistence and the use of your creative imagination will beat or overcome resistance **every** time.

And, along the way, slow down or stop to appreciate what you already have!

https://reecepye.com/blog/f/sometimes-it-pays-to-slow-down---the-power-of-gratitude

This is coming to the END of this book but the START of your new journey!

PURPOSE FOR A MEANINGFUL LIFE!

Purpose encompasses a person's sense of resolve or determination. It's stronger than any individual goal or objective because they take into account the broader picture, the complete person.

It's a powerful force for deciding on your ambitions, your personal standards and code of conduct, essentially how you will live your life now and ultimately, who you intend to become. Nobody can tell us the answer to what our purpose here on earth should be because it's the choice of each and every individual alive. For me right now, it's about enjoying life one day at a time and part of my enjoyment is seeing others becoming happier and more prosperous so that they in turn can help others, it's a ripple effect that goes far and wide.

What's your overriding purpose and how will you use the 7 steps to live it?

I'm sure many of you reading this have heard of Simon Sinek and his book **Start With Why?** Well, I'd like to **'End With Why'** and my reason for this is very important. If your 'why' for making improvements and changes in the way you manage your mind and achieve what you want in life is not strong enough, then your actions will not be strong enough to follow through.

My parting question is therefore a telling one for you and one you must answer honestly: ***Is the personal effort you're willing to put into (invest in) this 'self-coaching' program worth the rewards you will gain as a result?***

When and if you answer 'yes' to this question, you then need to follow the yes with another 'why' and be very clear about the strength of the reasons, the motives, the desires, the values that will be satisfied.

With that said, I now wish you Good Luck in managing and fully using the Miracle Power of Your Mind!

Yours Positively,

Reece

Printed in Great Britain
by Amazon